# THE BBC RADIOPHONIC WORKSHOP

## THE FIRST 25 YEARS

*R. W. Lambert*

Desmond Briscoe's first contact with Radio was as a performer in *Children's Hour*; he joined the BBC in 1941 and was one of those whose experiments led to the setting-up of the Radiophonic Workshop in 1958. A founder member, he was, in 1960, the first person appointed to direct and develop the Workshop. Whilst serving as Head of Radiophonic Workshop he has also produced experimental radio programmes, and in 1977 received three awards including the 'Gold' award for an outstanding contribution to radio.

Roy Curtis-Bramwell's keen interest in music and avant-garde poetry first brought him into contact with the Radiophonic Workshop in 1970. A Fleet Street journalist and specialist writer in the British film industry, he spent fifteen years with the BBC and was involved with BBC Records promotion and sleeve design for five formative years before moving to commercial television and freelance writing.

# THE BBC RADIOPHONIC WORKSHOP

## THE FIRST 25 YEARS

The inside story of providing sound and music
for television and radio 1958–1983

remembered by

DESMOND BRISCOE
and those whose versatility and unremitting
voluntary enthusiasm have made an idea a reality

realised by

ROY CURTIS-BRAMWELL

BRITISH BROADCASTING CORPORATION

The BBC Radiophonic Workshop provides a service of radiophonic
sound and music for television and radio.

We are often asked for sounds that have never been heard before.

We have prospered because we have provided them – more than
five thousand commitments over twenty-five years, realised on
anything and everything from the most advanced synthesiser/computer
in the world to a red fire extinguisher, in approximately G sharp.

Alternative titles for this book might also have been . . .
A CHORUS OF GLOW-WORMS
A HALO OF BEES
AN EASTER EGG FACTORY RUN BY RABBITS
A MONSTER CHOMPING ON ITS PREY
A HIGH HUM OF PURE AGONY
A GOTHIC ALTARPIECE
or even
BRINGING HOME THE BACON
(vide Francis Bacon's *New Atlantis* written in 1624)


This book is dedicated to Geoffrey Manuel,
Head of Programme Operations, Radio (Retired) in recognition
of his many years of encouragement and supportive administration.

*Desmond Briscoe, Head of the Radiophonic Workshop.*

Published by the British Broadcasting Corporation
35 Marylebone High Street, London W1M 4AA

ISBN 0 563 20150 9
First published 1983
© The contributors and the British Broadcasting Corporation 1983

Set in 11/13pt Monophoto Photina
and printed in England by BAS Printers Limited,
Over Wallop, Hampshire

# Contents

# Introduction

by Marghanita Laski

Most new inventions start as feeble imitations of what they will eventually supersede. The first printed books looked like manuscript writing. Both steam locomotives and internal combustion engines pulled horseless carriages. Man-made dress fabrics unconvincingly imitated natural ones, and plastics, with immense potential for a new kind of beauty, were bent to garishly-coloured copies of existing artefacts. And radio began by providing only such a world as a blind person might care to hear, and television only such a world as a stay-at-home might like to see.

But just like photography (another craft that began by copying art and later began to explore its own potential for art itself), radio and television soon began to serve not only the blind, actual and metaphorical, and not only the stay-at-homes, but listeners and viewers who were ready to accept from a new medium entirely new kinds of communications. Among these, both in its own right, and as a servant as miraculous as Aladdin's genie, came radiophonic sound.

It was in the late 1950s that some of us became aware of radiophonic sound, and at first in a negative sense. Something nasty that used to happen was happening far less often.

I concentrate on listeners because I myself prefer listening to viewing, and the something nasty that was happening less often was the use of 'real' music for brainwashing us into such moods of receptiveness as the programme producers wanted to induce in us. A snatch of Bach to introduce a brains trust, or of Boccherini for a lighter quiz; a fragment of Wagner for a ghostly visitation or of Johann Strauss for a ballroom floor. These practices had been maddening, impertinent and sometimes blasphemous. But in the fifties they were being replaced by new kinds of sounds. And so it was that those of us who were interested became aware of the BBC's Radiophonic Workshop which had started up as a sound-making service in 1958 after some promising experimentation a couple of years earlier.

By that time radio had already opened our ears to its capacity to bring us far more than the 'real' world of the blind. Already through experimental constructions which were still called – for want of a new name – plays, radio had shown itself to be a medium that could communicate a new and distinctive form of art, an art that could no more have existed before radio was invented than scribes could write typefaces or horses draw articulated coaches or painters catch actuality on the wing. Now, we began to realise, we were not only being spared the degradations of music misued. We were hearing deliberately created combinations of sound that had never existed in the world before.

So far as I was concerned, the first positive impact of radiophonic sound was that it was *sensational* – and by sensational, I mean it had a discernible physical impact. You can fairly say that all music is in this sense sensational, if you listen to it fully, and so, to some extent, it is. Plainsong, for example, balances musical and physical effect. Now this new sound-cum-music was providing physical sensations, and sometimes these were immensely interesting, immensely exciting, and, moreover, capable of being enhanced when experienced as a solitary sensation received stereophonically through headphones.

Radiophonic sound is also used as a means of identification – this is such-and-such a station, such-and-such a programme; or it provides interval sounds – don't ring up the BBC, your set isn't broken; or atmospheric sounds – yes, of course that was Major Bloodnok's stomach exploding. I am not yet convinced that it has valuably extended the boundaries of 'real' music; indeed, I find that when the sounds proffered are nearest to 'real' music they are least valuable. This, I think, corresponds to radiophonics' period of copying rather than revolutionising.

That a still more useful future lies ahead we cannot doubt. Perhaps radiophonic sound will eventually come to replace the horrors of Muck Music where what is needed is rather rhythm than melody: on railway-station concourses, for instance, or airports, or for relieving boredom on motorways – though for this last purpose they must avoid sounds that might suggest that something is horribly wrong with the vehicle.

What Desmond Briscoe and his colleagues have so far achicved is marvellous, and of those achievements this book is a worthy chronicle. Shall the next instalment of history be able to tell us how from these marvels, this brilliance of ingenuity, there emerged, at last, a new kind of real music, a new development of the highest form of art we yet know?

# CHAPTER 1
## *Private Dreams*

'I have seen a dream come true – almost.
I still marvel that it ever happened'
*Desmond Briscoe*

*Left:* Members of the
Radiophonic Workshop in 1983.
From left to right: Brian
Hodgson, Elizabeth Parker, Jon
Gibbs, Dick Mills, Peter Howell,
Roger Limb, Desmond Briscoe
(sitting)

*Below:* The BBC music studios in
Maida Vale, formerly the Maida
Vale Roller Skating Palace and
Club

The Royal Borough of Westminster stretches surprisingly far north of
the River Thames to include Maida Vale which is a rather respectable
suburb. It was here that the not altogether respectable music and sound
first pioneered in Europe as *musique concrète* and electronic music were
united with the needs of the BBC, and emerged as radiophonic music
and sound. It amazed, annoyed and entertained the British listening
and viewing public for the next twenty-five years. Maida Vale has wide
streets and a lot of mellow red brick and white stucco. The houses that
once provided grand homes for Edwardian families, now form a leafy
bedsitterland where you can buy a picture on a floating art gallery or
take a narrow boat on the Regent's Canal to London Zoo.

The BBC first came here in the mid 1930s, looking for a quiet area
and a building large enough to house a music studio centre. It found
both in Delaware Road in what was formerly The Maida Vale Roller

Skating Palace and Club, a floridly baroque/art-nouveau part of the
1909 development of the area. One of the largest and most sumptuous
rinks of the day, its sunken floor gave hundreds of skaters the room to
twist and turn; and a balcony enabled spectators to take afternoon tea
and look down on the skaters below whilst the Palace Band played
waltzes of the day.

Thirty-six grand pianos representing nineteen different makes, assembled in the big BBC studio at Maida Vale

When the BBC took over, the resident band was replaced by a greatly
multiplied army of musicians: members of the BBC Symphony
Orchestra, the Chamber Music Groups, and all the popular dance bands
of the 'thirties. They played in one or other of the studios formed from
the roller-rink, and the music they made downstairs was relayed to the
former spectators' gallery, now converted to recording rooms. These
were the rooms which were to become, one by one, the home of a
unique experimental studio – the BBC Radiophonic Workshop.

In moving into Room 13, built on the former spectators' gallery, the
Radiophonic Workshop had displaced a machine which had a
formidable reputation as a sort of dinosaur of sound recording – the
Blattnerphone. The rare examples of the machine that still exist no longer
offer the risk of instantly decapitating anyone within reach of its whirling
steel tape. Children who come across the Science Museum's machine
regard it with awe, comparing its bulk with their own personal recorder
held in the hand as easily as a box of chocolates.

The Blattnerphone, monstrous by modern microchip standards, nevertheless performed the job it was intended to do; it recorded programmes to be broadcast later, rather than when they happened. In its own way it was the professional broadcasting successor to the hurdy-gurdies, barrel-organs, parlour pianos, phonograph cylinders and gramophone records.

Steel tape gave way to direct recording on disc, which was eventually replaced by tape of ferrous-covered plastic, and a new breed of tape-recorder. As these recorders came into use, broadcasters realised that entirely new techniques were possible. Not only could the new machines record and replay, but the tape could be easily cut up and manipulated. Sound became a malleable object.

The Blattnerphone with its reel of steel tape

Whereas the Blattnerphone's 22-lb reels had whirled steel tape around at a frightening speed, and the recording engineers sheltered in a little room next door in case the tape broke and hundreds of feet of very live steel thrashed ungovernably about, the new tape could be edited with razor blade and sticky tape. The previous method was to weld it back together on an anvil. Recording engineers in the Blattnerphone days were blacksmiths as well as soundsmiths.

The new soundsmiths were mainly BBC producers and studio managers who had been inspired by the new sounds radiating from Paris and Cologne. In Broadcasting House and another BBC studio in Piccadilly, they worked, mostly at night when the broadcasts of the day were over and they could get at the facilities they needed.

The story of how a young French Broadcaster, Pierre Schaeffer, discovered what he was later to call 'musique concrète' may well be apocryphal. He is said to have been broadcasting from an underground radio station at the time of the Liberation. The needle stuck in the groove of an Edith Piaf record, and then started up again. That sound encouraged Schaeffer to pursue 'the music in between'; to perform similar experiments and then to record natural sounds and change their nature through a multiplicity of operations. Apocryphal or not, there is no doubt that he was the guiding light of the movement. The advent of tape-recording was a major breakthrough: Schaeffer created his 'phonogene' machine, which enabled control of the pitch and speed of his natural sounds. Pierre Henri, his close colleague, was commissioned to compose this new music to accompany texts, ballets, films and an opera.

In Germany, the experimenters at the Nord Deutsche Rundfunk broadcasting studios in Cologne concentrated on using synthetic sound sources, naming the music they finally evolved elektronische Musik. Unlike musique concrète, notoriously difficult to score, the electronic music from Cologne could be planned as a composition right from the start.

In Italy a laboratory set up by the country's broadcasting organisation under Luciano Berio combined both elements. Experiments were also in progress at the Philips Research Laboratory in Eindhoven, Holland, and at several studios in America.

Wherever they may have worked, and in whatever particular form of the 'new music', experimenters tended to be secretive about their working methods. The result of their labours, when performed at public concerts or in broadcasts, were so much at the sharp end of the vanguard that the ordinary public generally responded with stunned silence followed by howls of abuse. Critics were kinder, though guarded. If there was a camaraderie in those early experimental days it was that of self-preservation, either in agreeing to collectively duck heads to avoid the abuse, or to proclaim that all new pioneering work suffered from mistrust, misunderstanding and downright condemnation.

History has, after all, proved them to have been right and their detractors wrong!

The new music appealed to the BBC not so much as an art form in its own right, but in the way in which it could be used to enhance the sound of radio drama. No longer content with stock sound from the Library, a handful of producers and studio managers were now prepared for something quite different.

Experimentation with sound was in the air, not only for serious drama and the more avant-garde works, but also for comedy where comics and their producers and writers had long ago realised the importance of the auditory cliché. Tommy Handley's famous *ITMA* door – which opened to allow the character to say his or her lines and then closed on their departure – was almost an *ITMA* character itself. Long before there was a Radiophonic Workshop *The Goon Show* had developed sound into extended aural cliff-hangers which usually lasted much longer than anyone had expected, starting up again after a pause as if to say 'we're not done yet'. Footsteps took forever to approach, pass by, and fade away into the distance. Even when speeded up, they were stylised and uniquely Goonish. The *Goon Show* fall or disaster was a memorable aural event – an avalanche of sounds which crashed down onto a level thousands of feet below; paused; then started off again to the final agonising thud, clump or clank.

All these stylised sounds were a move forward from the past towards something new. It so happened that they were moving towards Room 13 at Maida Vale, where the BBC would eventually open a small experimental workshop for the production of 'radiophonic' sound and music.

That was to come about in April 1958, but more than twelve months previously, a number of people within the BBC were already experimenting with sounds stemming directly from *musique concrète*. The enthusiasts included producers John Gibson, Douglas Cleverdon, Donald McWhinnie and Michael Bakewell; writer/producer Frederick Bradnum and playwright Giles Cooper; studio managers Daphne Oram, Desmond Briscoe and Norman Bain.

Daphne Oram, a prime mover in the cause, was a trained engineer and musician. Her private researches and experiments had previously led her to try and persuade both BBC Engineers and programme makers that the Corporation should be taking seriously the development, composition and presentation of electronic music.

The first collaboration of consequence for the new experimenters was nevertheless for Samuel Beckett's *All That Fall*, an important radio play specially written for the BBC and broadcast in the Third Programme in 1957. It was the first programme to contain what later came to be known as 'radiophonic' sound, and is acknowledged as one of radio's classic productions.

*All That Fall*, the first of Beckett's plays to be written originally in English, came about when Donald McWhinnie visited the renowned playwright at his Paris home and discovered him to be enthusiastic about experimentation in sound. Beckett was one of the biggest literary figures of the day, whose plays were considered avant-garde but meaningful. McWhinnie's success in persuading him to write specially for BBC radio was an achievement matched only by the response when the script was duly delivered in 1956: it was a work of genius, but one that tested the ingenuity of the producer and the practicalities of the medium.

*All That Fall* was a script that obviously called for very special sound treatment. Donald McWhinnie talked to the only man in the BBC with a known shared interest and enthusiasm for such a task, someone who also had the technical know-how of how it could be achieved: Desmond Briscoe.

Born in Birkenhead, Desmond Briscoe had come to radio very young indeed. When he first broadcast as a child on *Children's Hour* in Manchester he knew that he wanted to become involved eventually as a professional. He was also a percussionist and ran a dance band from a very early age, so he knew a bit about the entertainment business from the musician's point of view.

I kept applying to join the BBC and they kept saying 'Come back when you are older', so I went away and came back when I was older until eventually they gave me an interview, ostensibly with the BBC Engineering Department because I had done science at school. When they asked me about Ohm's Law, and I couldn't tell them correctly what it was, they explained that there were people called Programme Engineers and that I had better become one of them because they were the people that looked after sound effects and the balance of music and that sort of thing where a knowledge of Ohm's Law wasn't quite so essential!

Right from the start I was involved with the big dramatic radio features of the time. Radio for its own sake meant so much to Features Department, and I was fortunate that when I joined, in 1941, I was working with such people as Geoffrey Bridson, Stephen Potter, Laurence Gilliam, Cecil McGivern, Louis MacNeice and Joan Littlewood. I had tried so hard for so long to get into the BBC; now that I was working there I couldn't believe my good fortune in finding myself in such company.

*Right:* Desmond Briscoe

Radio features in those days were ambitious, interesting and
original pieces of radio that demanded and received total
commitment from those involved. Apart from these productions, I
did sound effects for drama, and became more and more involved
with music programmes. It was then that I first became aware of the
way that sound and music might come together.

Called up for wartime service, Desmond left the BBC to serve with the
Grenadier Guards. It was, he says, 'a terrible mistake for them and
certainly for me'. Nevertheless, being stationed at Windsor Castle, he
had important duties which included looking after the safety of the
Royal Family, one of whom he was destined to meet again in 1971, when
Her Majesty The Queen attended a presentation of radiophonic music at
the Royal Festival Hall.

Later in his Army career he transferred from the Guards to the Royal
Army Educational Corps and into work which was more appropriate to
his temperament and abilities. It was while lecturing on music
appreciation that he met a Welsh ATS girl named Gwyneth who was
later to become his wife. Together they served in India until the end of
1947, and then returned to England for demobilisation.

The Briscoes settled in London and Desmond rejoined the BBC at
Broadcasting House making sound effects for radio drama.

After seven years of not having moved up the ladder, and at an
interview to discuss his career, he recounted his army experiences:
guarding the Royal Family at Windsor; Music Adviser for Education,
London District Command; teaching at the Vice-Regal Lodge in Simla –
to say nothing of exploring the mountains and lakes of Kashmir.

The Personnel Officer finally remarked: 'You had a most interesting
war, Mr Briscoe, but you can't expect the rest of life to be like that.'
Desmond reacted characteristically and took that as a challenge!

Tape machines, which had existed during the war in Germany, were
now becoming available in England and a few were used by the BBC for
rehearsal purposes. Seeing the broadcaster Desmond Carrington taking
extracts on tape from the sound track of films to link with narrative to
produce radio versions of movies, Briscoe was suddenly aware that tape
was an object of considerable potential. 'You could cut it up with
scissors and join the pieces together. Suddenly sound on tape was for
me an entirely different thing with limitless possibilities.'

Nevertheless, as a studio manager responsible for sound effects, he
was working very much in the traditional manner, going to the BBC
Sound Effects Library and choosing what he wanted.

The BBC had a very large library of natural sounds, but some of
the discs were distinctly odd in that they played from the middle
outwards rather than the other way around. If you put the pick-
up on the usual starting position it just fell off.

Studio 2 Piccadilly where *All That Fall* and other early radiophonic productions were made

When I was doing sound effects on 'grams' I might well have six or eight turntables to operate at one time. Some records would spiral inwards and some outwards, and the trick was to remember which! Naturally I began to understand how to mix sounds together in order to create a complex sound picture – and this was, I suppose, where my understanding of the techniques and possibilities offered by tape arose.

Though we didn't realise it then, round about this time was a golden age of radio, and I was part of it. Music and drama came together for me in a very original and adventurous way. I was fortunate once again in working with so many talented producers. Some of them had been in radio for many years and were extremely distinguished in their careers. Others were comparative new boys encouraging a new kind of writer and new styles of making radio drama.

I was interested in experimental work, so I naturally gravitated to the people who were pioneering the new things whenever I could. I suppose that's why Donald McWhinnie asked my advice about that script by Samuel Beckett, *All That Fall*.

*All That Fall* was broadcast in the BBC Third Programme in

1957, and proved a classic of its kind. It has been revered in radio circles ever since as a rare and important experiment carried out between one of Europe's foremost writers, and the BBC in its more experimental mood. It is one of the key programmes of the golden age of radio drama, and – incorrectly – has entered the official catalogues of electronic music as the first British production to contain electronic music. In point of fact the sounds in *All That Fall* were created from concrete sources, and there was no electronic element at all. What little music there was came from ordinary gramophone records subjected to radiophonic treatment.

But for the team involved in its making, *All That Fall* was a production that enabled them to use the new possibilities of sound manipulation as if it were a new toy.

Beckett's script was remarkable, really remarkable, says Desmond Briscoe. He wrote 'silence' and 'pause', quite obviously differentiating between the two. When he demanded sounds, he didn't say they had to be made in any particular way, but the whole nature of the script led to experimentation.

Eventually we did away with natural sounds altogether, and simulated – for instance – the sounds of people walking with a simple drum rhythm.

I taught the studio manager what we wanted. The natural footsteps would be blended into the drums in exactly the same rhythm. It was all done live in the studio. The new techniques were fascinating: when we faded up the replay knob of the recording machine while it was still recording, we produced tape feed-back. This is now the tried and trusty technique usually known as 'flutter-echo'. We had heard the sound before on records of *musique concrète* – it wasn't our invention – but it was the first time that we had used it on radio drama. It was particularly good for suggesting that slightly 'fantasy feeling' of things happening in a larger-than-life way. For example, when the 'Up-Mail' train hurtles through the sleepy station, the effect was heightened by all the sounds clattering and reiterating.

*All That Fall* consists of a string of episodes set in the Irish suburb of Boghill 'around noon on a Saturday of changeable weather'. The world is that of Beckett's own childhood – Protestant, middleclass, concerned with religion and horse-racing. There are touches which place it in the past: 'A penny is an appropriate tip to a helpful boy . . . and seven and sixpence a day enough to keep a man alive and twitching'.

*All That Fall* was rated quite a success within the BBC, and many listeners were impressed. What the majority of the British public thought of it is not known, but one schoolmaster certainly wrote to the BBC to protest about 'this bloody pretentious trash!'

In the same year, 1957, Giles Cooper's *The Disagreeable Oyster* was broadcast and showed that the radiophonic experimenters could also be funny – something that was to surprise those critics who associated radiophonic sound exclusively with nightmares, horror and madness.

Giles Stannus Cooper (1918–1966) did not, like Louis MacNeice, Dylan Thomas or Samuel Beckett, bring a famous literary name to Broadcasting House. He began his career as an actor-turned-dramatist for the theatre, becoming involved with radio during the 1940s. He began immediately to experiment, the complexity of his plays increasing markedly with *Mathry Beacon* in 1956, and persisting through a variety of experiments in the late 'fifties which included the two 'radiophonic plays' – *The Disagreeable Oyster* and *Under the Loofah Tree*. Both these plays, together with Beckett's *All That Fall*, have been remade and broadcast again in recent years by Desmond Briscoe.

*The Disagreeable Oyster* is about a man who goes up to the north of England on a business trip armed with an expense account and freedom from his wife. The world might be his oyster, but it turns out to be a surrealist world where he experiences a series of exaggerated cartoon-like encounters. It is an ideal radio play in that its auditory setting is as substantial as it is treacherous.

Donald McWhinnie, who originally produced the play, said in his *Art of Radio*: 'The radio act comes out of silence, vibrates in the void and in the mind, and returns to silence, like music. ... because of the conditions governing its existence, structure is of prime importance to radio, as it is to music ... ' This quote echoes Samuel Beckett's own comment on his script of *All That Fall*: 'It is a text written to come out of the dark.' *The Disagreeable Oyster* required a great deal of the developing radiophonic skills to create the sounds specified on Cooper's shopping list of auditory effects. Donald McWhinnie looks back with affection on the making of these plays: 'I remember that Desmond and I spent many pleasant hours experimenting and fiddling about. At that time it was all sporadic hit and miss. We were part of a small minority of perhaps half a dozen people who responded immediately and thought that radio-phonic plays were fun. Maybe we regarded ourselves as slightly eccentric, but we enjoyed doing it.'

*The Disagreeable Oyster* had a slightly Goonish humour, and contained one effect that the Goons had made famous: high-speed footsteps.

We used them because they seemed appropriate, certainly not because the Goons had used them, says Desmond Briscoe. Incidentally, the only way to make high-speed footsteps in those days was to force the turntable round with your finger as fast as possible. The engineers didn't really approve of this because it did no good to the governing mechanism of the turntable.

Everything we did for Giles Cooper's plays was an experiment. We knew, of course, that ultimately we had to go into a booked studio and make the actual programme, but the run-up to this often involved extended days because when the day ran out we just carried on at night.

When we made the programme, though it was recorded, it was mixed in one continuous 'take'. Michael Bakewell came to watch me mixing and said afterwards that it was like watching someone play Liszt on the piano. Lance Sieveking has spoken about 'playing' the dramatic control panel, and Val Gielgud in his book said the same thing. That's what it is – you have all the sound sources there and you play them. You perform.

Another Donald McWhinnie programme, *Private Dreams and Public Nightmares*, lasted only twelve minutes, was broadcast only once on the Third Programme in October 1957, but was destined to bring the word 'radiophonic' to the public attention for the first time.

It was subsequently issued by the BBC Transcription Service and has been broadcast in many countries throughout the world. Not very long ago it had another airing in the USA, where listeners were amazed that it had been made so long ago and with the very primitive facilities available in the late 'fifties.

A pre-Radiophonic Workshop photograph of Daphne Oram and Frederick Bradnum, author of *Private Dreams and Public Nightmares*. Daphne Oram is playing a loop in a studio at Broadcasting House

The programme was made by Daphne Oram, Desmond Briscoe, Norman Bain, Donald McWhinnie and others who worked day and night, mostly in Piccadilly Two, a studio which had been a stage door canteen during the war and which was favoured by the radiophonic experimenters because, unlike the studios at Broadcasting House, Piccadilly Two had its own recording room. This meant that with collaborative recording engineers, all sorts of exciting things were possible.

The BBC was aware of the potential of radiophonic sound and music and had set up a committee to ponder the issue. This one programme was to ensure that the experimenters were given at least the basic necessities for furthering their dreams.

*Private Dreams and Public Nightmares* was written by Frederick Bradnum. It was subtitled 'A Radiophonic Poem', and like Beckett's script for *All That Fall*, it was written with sound in mind. But in this case the sounds required were specified on one side of the page, and the poem on the other. Nothing quite like it had ever been seen before.

It followed various tentative experiments made by the BBC over the previous years by composers such as Humphrey Searle and Roberto Gerhard and producers such as Douglas Cleverdon and John Gibson, and was a first positive attempt to compose a radio programme specifically designed to exploit the new sounds and entirely dependent on them for effect. It begins:

| *Basic Effects* | | *Dialogue* |
|---|---|---|
| A contrapuntal rhythm. | IST VOICE: | Round and round |
| | | Like a wind from the ground |
| | | Deep and deep |
| | | A world turns in sleep. |
| A comet-like shriek. | 2ND VOICE: | I fall through nothing, vast, empty spaces. |
| Acoustic change. | | Darkness and the pulse of my life bound, |
| Pulsating beat. | | |
| Descending scale. | | Intertwined with the pulse of the dark world. |
| A developed sound like a cry. | | Still falling, falling, But slower now. . . . |

Donald McWhinnie explained in his book *The Art of Radio* that it was 'an inextricable conception of word and special sound and an exploratory flight into a new territory of sound. The words were designed to evoke, and be reinforced by, new sounds, sounds never heard before, and to be themselves subjected to technical processes which would achieve emotional effects (with the human voice as basis) quite different from anything the actor can do on his own'.

Before it went out on the air, the BBC circulated a warning note to the engineers who monitored the quality of broadcast sound. It said, in effect: 'Don't attempt to alter anything that sounds strange – it's deliberately meant to sound that way.'

In order that the public should not be alarmed, McWhinnie called a press listening session when he explained just what was being attempted. This explanation also formed the introduction to the BBC transcription service recording sent to other broadcasters overseas. It reads:

This programme is an experiment – an exploration. It's been put together with enormous enthusiasm and equipment designed for other purposes. It's not a masterpiece, not even a minor one, and it's not a stunt. We think it's worth broadcasting as a perfectly serious first attempt to find out whether we can convey a new kind of emotional and intellectual experience by means of what we call radiophonic effects.

By radiophonic effects, we mean something very near to what the French have labelled *musique concrète* – concrete music. Not music at all really. It doesn't necessarily come out of musical instruments and it can't be written down. It's simply sound, or patterns of sound, which are manufactured by technical processes. The basis of it is an unlimited supply of magnetic tape, recording machine, razor blade and something to stick the bits together with, and a group of technicians who think nothing is too much trouble, provided it works.

You take a sound – any sound – record it, and then change its nature by a multiplicity of operations. You record it at different speeds, you play it backwards, you add it to itself over and over again. You adjust filters, echoes, acoustic qualities. You combine segments of magnetic tape. By these means and many others you can create sounds which no one has ever heard before. Sounds which have an indefinable and unique quality of their own. You can compose a vast and subtle symphony from the noise of a pin dropping. In fact, one of the most vibrant and elemental sounding noises in tonight's programme started life as an extremely tinny cow bell.

It's a sort of modern magic. Many of you may be familiar with it – they've been exploiting it on the Continent for years – but strangely enough we've held aloof, partly through distrust – is it simply a new toy? – partly through complacency, ignorance too. But we're saying at last that we think there's something in it, but we aren't calling it *musique concrète* – in fact, we've decided not to use the word music at all.

Some musicians believe that it can become an art form complete in itself, others are sceptical. That's not our immediate concern. We're interested in its application to radio writing, dramatic or poetic – adding a new dimension – a form which is essentially radio.

Properly used, radiophonic effects have no near relationship with any existing sound. They're free of irrelevant associations. They have an emotional life of their own and they could be a new and invaluable strand in the texture of radio and theatre and cinema and television.

Frederick Bradnum has given us a text specifically designed to exploit some of these new sounds and dependent on them for full effect.

The sub-title is A Radiophonic Poem. We believe that such an art form may exist, quite distinct from the poem on the page or the poem read aloud. A poetic experience which only exists in terms of a sound complex. And the programme isn't a model – it simply tries to indicate the sort of possibilities that are within reach and I'm not suggesting that your ears should now be bombarded by programmes of this kind. There are any number of ways of using these new techniques. They've already been applied in a modest way in thrillers and science fiction plays. Indeed, the broad effects are the easiest to achieve – horror, hysterical comedy. It's much more difficult to manage tenderness, lyrical beauty, sweetness and light – perhaps because of the inhuman element in the actual process of manufacture. But I do believe that many writers will find an imaginative stimulus in this demonstration of a new mode of expression, a new adjunct to the spoken word and, as we learn more and improve our equipment, the possibilities will increase.

An African Piano. This one is made from bicycle spokes

One thought does occur from time to time – not entirely frivolously – would it not be more illuminating to play the whole thing backwards?

After the broadcast, reactions were mixed. The critic on *The Times* disagreed with McWhinnie's remark about playing the whole thing backwards. Though he didn't think that highly of the programme, he did applaud the fact that it gave English listeners the opportunity of hearing the actual sounds of *musique concrète* rather than just the argument against them. The programme demonstrated 'its power to support, indeed to transfigure, the most commonplace writing'. *The Observer* was more enthusiastic: 'Its possibilities, as some of last week's shrieks and reverberations showed, are tremendous for anyone willing to treat it as a standard means of accompanying the right kind of play or feature' while *The Guardian* decided that 'the conclusion one came to after what was certainly a strange and rather unpleasant immersion in sounds cleverly calculated to affect the mind and feeling, was that the technique could be brilliantly used in illustration (as to a certain extent it always has been) but that it would not give a radio masterpiece to the world unless the text were the most important'. The *Daily Telegraph*, referring to 'Horror on the Third', gave a hint of things to come: 'The BBC is spending £2000 on equipment and setting up a team to exploit the possibilities of the idea for imaginative writers.'

Whatever else the programme had achieved, it had brought the setting up of a permanent Radiophonic Workshop that much nearer. As Frederick Bradnum says: 'The group of people who made the programme were the real people whom we can thank for keeping the whole interest going. They were all dedicated to finding out just what could technically be done. When it came to setting up the Workshop they had a hell of a battle all down the line.'

Drawing by Gerard Hoffnung from *Hoffnung's Acoustics*

# CHAPTER 2
## *Public Nightmares*

'If you are certain you are the victim of a neighbouring oscillator,
co-operate with your friends in an endeavour to locate the
offender . . . many an elusive oscillator has been caught by being
observed when he sends his accumulator to be charged or when he
goes away on holiday . . .'
*BBC Leaflet 1930s*

The word 'oscillation', when applied to early radio, meant the very
nasty noise that resulted when tuning in a valve set. After long periods
of patiently tuning in through bursts of hiss and static and eventually
settling down to listen to the programme, it must have been intensely
irritating to have that programme drowned out by the howling
oscillations of a neighbour who was also fiddling with his tuning.

In the early 'twenties the BBC enlisted the help of the Post Office to try
to cut down the annoyance. Post Office motor vans drove slowly about
the streets being as conspicuous as possible with the intention of
intimidating, rather than detecting, 'the neighbouring oscillator'.

During the General Strike, the BBC became very seriously worried
when strikers threatened to interfere with their programmes through
'wholesale oscillation'. All in all, oscillation was a nasty and
unwelcome noise to most people.

But not to the experimenters in radiophonic sound. The possibilities of
using such sounds to generate electronic music had been recognised and
realised, particularly by post-war experimenters in Cologne.

In 1954, the BBC radio serial *Journey into Space* incorporated the
recorded sounds of tones from oscillators passed through the National
Physical Laboratory's reverberation chamber for a lone and early
venture into 'spacey' sounds.

Perhaps typically, it was to be the newly formed Radiophonic
Workshop that would take the much-disliked oscillations to use in a
symbolic way: as a rainbow of sound leading (hopefully) away from the
nightmares of the past. The name of the play, appropriately enough,
was *Noah*, and Desmond Briscoe and Jimmy Burnett created the sounds
in 1958, some six months after the Workshop was opened.

Not that the dreaded oscillators had been tamed and were suddenly
cuddly and lovable. The nightmares of the past were now the
nightmares of the present day as far as many listeners and critics were
concerned. Phrases used in protest included: 'The radiophonic sound

just added to the psychological confusion' . . . 'Obscure and distracting' . . . 'a neurotic gimmick for infantile listeners' . . . 'maddening and hideous' . . . 'beaten to death by radiophonic bumps and grinds'.

Apparently for many people the oscillators were still making horrible sounds. The difference was that they were now *meant* to be horrible sounds which were created in order to disturb in the name of entertainment. At least the Radiophonic Workshop had exonerated 'the neighbours', who promptly got together to write letters to the *Radio Times* and *The Listener* against their common enemy.

It was to take another five years before the oscillators – or 'electronic sound generators' – were to be finally accepted in their new role. In 1963 a Workshop composer called Delia Derbyshire realised by a series of 'carefully timed hand-swoops' on twelve small oscillators the signature tune for a new children's series called *Doctor Who*. The story of how this momentous event came about is described in chapter 8.

Brian Hodgson with a wobbulator, (left) a bank of oscillators, a keyboard controller and frequency counter. These made the Workshop's electronic sounds before the advent of the synthesisers

But before Noah's aural rainbow or indeed any other sounds could come from the about-to-be-born infant, the Radiophonic Workshop's gestation period was proving lengthy and wordy.

It was in November 1956 that the BBC first seriously entered the field of natural-cum-electronic sound following earlier 'active investigations'. Head of Central Programme Operations, Brian George, was principally concerned with the technical facilities required to enable the BBC to keep pace with the developments elsewhere in the field of electronic sound effects. Much was written on the subject, and no doubt the files would have been even thicker had it not been for the impetus given by a report from Donald McWhinnie of his visit to meet the *musique concrète* pioneers in Paris.

The Club d'Essai, part of the Radio-Télévision Française broadcasting organisation, proved to be an exciting place – even though the original team headed by Pierre Schaeffer and Pierre Henri was now somewhat rift with internecine feuds. 'The Club provided', wrote McWhinnie on his return, 'a special approach to actors and radio "performance" and to aural inventiveness through *musique concrète*, acoustic effects and the highly imaginative use of sheer sound. It could not 'fail to prove stimulating to an enthusiast for the medium'.

Though not impressed by the scripts the French were working with McWhinnie reported that

in their handling of sound they are miles ahead, although their expertise is often lavished indiscriminately and to the point of absurdity on trivial subjects. I would not for a moment suggest a similar research set-up here, or even an equal preoccupation with 'noises', but there is no doubt in my mind that if we are seriously concerned with radio as a medium in its own right we cannot afford to neglect the development of this particular ingredient, and, indeed, should set out positively to profit from the Club d'Essai's experience.

McWhinnie proposed that the BBC first listened to French tapes, not in order to copy them, but for

the stimulus which they give and the possible development they suggest. (Following talks at departmental meetings I gather that a number of producers are already anxious to have a practical demonstration.)

Secondly, it means obtaining facilities for private experiment and for making recordings which may never be broadcast. Clearly the exact requirements would have to be worked out in detail with a technical expert and in consultation with the Club d'Essai: I should say that the basic essentials would be a room containing two or three tape reproduction machines, turntables for slow speed of 78s, a tape-recorder, facilities for echo, filters, etc., and a small studio with two or three microphone points, an old piano, various percussive instruments and space for two or three actors.

In December 1956, the 'Electrophonic Effects Committee' had met to investigate:

a) The facilities required to set up a combined technical and operational 'workshop' to provide electrophonic effects as supporting sound for certain programmes.

b) Subject to approval of the recommendations, to direct and develop the output of the 'workshop'.

The committee agreed that the most descriptive name for the finished product was 'Electrophonic Effects' – but they soon changed their minds when in January 1957 it was pointed out that 'electrophonic' was an expression in current use in brain and hearing scientific research.

In March 1957, the committee met as 'The Radiophonic Effects Committee' to define their terms, talk about accommodation and the equipment needed if such a venture was to get off the ground. Two large rooms were certainly necessary, and even at this stage a scouting party had looked at Maida Vale but reported back that suitable rooms were not available. Hottest favourite for workshop accommodation at that time was Nightingale Square, south of the river in Balham, the home of a section of the Engineering Division.

Douglas Cleverdon was one of the most influential producers in Features Department who had made the original production of Dylan Thomas's *Under Milk Wood*. He was also one of the prime movers of the Radiophonic Workshop's cause, his interest in *musique concrète* stemming from his first-hand experience of the music made by several of his friends working in Paris. He was one of the first BBC producers to bring this experimental work to the ears of the British public, and also provided playbacks of *musique concrète* to invited audiences in the Council Chamber of Broadcasting House, and elsewhere, in order to create awareness of the new music among a wide range of BBC creative and administrative people. He recalls:

The Workshop in those days existed as an idea for those of us who were working for word reinforcement. Though the finest radio comes from poet's words . . . there are certain occasions when you wish to widen the range of the impact of the words with something else. . . In the pre-Workshop days a producer conveying his ideas to the studio manager sitting beside him wasn't very popular. We were pleased when the committee established to look into the setting up of a workshop could actually justify the institution of the Radiophonic Workshop – because it would save a lot of bother.

My attitude has always been that I was interested in music as an ingredient in radio and whatever would serve radio best was what I wanted, whether it was by orchestra, voices, sound effects, sounds, *musique concrète* or electronic music and sounds. I don't think that the Music Department in the BBC were particularly interested; they were concerned with transmitting music rather than initiating it, except to commission an occasional symphony. Most of the earlier experimentation came from Features Department and Drama under McWhinnie.

Val Gielgud, Head of Drama, was in favour of setting up the Workshop, but wondered whether the BBC could afford it. He wondered whether 'when economy is on everyone's lips', the expense could be justified. Also: 'The use of these electronic devices must be a limited one, and indeed it would be thoroughly bad if simply because the devices were at our disposal they should be used high wide and handsome . . .'

Head of Variety, Pat Hillyard, also queried whether the sums needed for the scheme could be justified, but added that 'Experiment in sound' was certainly something that would be welcomed by members of his department. Head of Features, Laurence Gilliam, came out 'strongly in favour of this development', and supported 'its immediate and rapid implementation'. 'I am,' he said, 'certain that this development is overdue as part of the BBC's equipment and that worthwhile programme results will materialise.'

The only caveat Gilliam imposed was that he considered the use of this type of equipment should be 'most stringently controlled by a small group of qualified producers, working with interested and qualified studio managers and musicians. In this way, the "lunatic fringe" of experimentalists could be restrained, and creative and worthwhile contributions to sound broadcasting made in a controlled manner'.

The moneys in question which had activated so many to such a flurry of correspondence from suggestion to decision was exactly £2000 'for minimum purchase of essential equipment not obtainable from redundant plant'.

By June 1957, the prospect of the Radiophonic Workshop having a Balham address had faded away, and they were definitely Maida Vale-bound. Brian George wrote to Senior Engineer Sound Broadcasting:

> We had almost given up hope of finding suitable accommodation for the Radiophonic Effects Unit and the area which you are kindly making available promises to meet the needs of the unit with the minimum expenditure on wiring, acoustic treatment, etc. I am very grateful.

The rooms were cleared during July, and the (mostly redundant) equipment transferred from various BBC premises into Maida Vale. It was a triumph for the Workshop's various supporters, some of whom were able to watch Room 13 being wired up. The actual opening day – 1 April 1958 – passed by unmarked by official events. In fact the whole place was in utter chaos for the first weeks and most of the days were spent in trying to make the equipment work, learning exactly what it could do when working, and coping with the constant stream of creative people eager to get on with the job of using the Workshop for programme making.

In May 1958, a month after the unit had opened its doors, the press were invited to visit. According to BBC Publicity Officer Michael Hardwick, the event was 'a considerable success'. Journalists came from *The Times, Telegraph, Birmingham Post, Glasgow Herald, New Scientist, Central Office of Information, PA Reuters News Agency, Journal of the Institute of Electrical Engineers, Journal of the British Institute of Recording Engineers, Practical Wireless, British Radio and Television, The Gramophone*, and *Wireless World and Engineering*.

The official BBC Press Release to mark the occasion began:

### BBC Opens Britain's First Radiophonic Workshop

The BBC has set up a Radiophonic Workshop at Maida Vale in London, the first installation of its kind in this country to deal exclusively with the production of radiophonic effects. Thus the BBC is now equipped to provide an aid to productions which neither music nor conventional sound effects can give.

The original Workshop in Room 13 and 14 at Maida Vale, with the original Workshop team: (from left to right) Donald McWhinnie is making notes on his script of a sound montage prepared by the staff of the Workshop; Daphne Oram is locating a specific sound, whilst a component tape is being edited by Desmond Briscoe. Richard ('Dickie') Bird is re-setting a cue on a tape of prepared sounds

What is radiophonic sound? It is a new sound – suggestive of emotion, sensation, mood, rather than the literal moaning of a wind or the opening of a door. Created by mechanical means from basic sounds which may vary from the rustle of paper to a note from an electronic oscillator, radiophonic sound provides the writer and producer with an entirely new field in which to convey his intentions with the utmost subtlety of expression.

Its functions are quite different from those of what is usually termed *musique concrète*, and although some of the techniques are similar radiophonic sound is not an art in itself – it is used to provide an additional 'dimension' for radio and television productions.

In setting up the Workshop, to provide a permanent centre for work of this kind, the choice of technical equipment has been determined by two categories into which radiophonic sounds

aphne Oram playing the
lijwiz while 'Dickie' Bird
ecords on the Motosacoche

mainly fall:

1) Those which can be built up from basic material of natural sounds – e.g. voices, bells, musical instruments, etc.

2) Those derived from wave-forms generated by electronic circuits – e.g. oscillator, white noise generators, etc.

The reporting of the event was mainly factual, with only two daily newspapers showing concern. The critic of *The Times* wrote, 'So far as one can judge, this is the only programme material put out by the BBC which sounds probably just as well played backwards'.

Whereas the *Daily Telegraph* offered slightly more hope for the future: 'None of these radiophonic noises seems to suggest anything but misery. Later on, say the BBC, they hope to produce something more cheerful'.

Not only was the BBC Radiophonic Workshop now open, and seen to be open, but it possessed what Douglas Cleverdon considered to be its greatest advantage: 'It started off as a collection of enthusiasts, and I think that is always the right way to start anything. The difficulty is to keep it going as a collection of enthusiasts and not a number of people who are just looking round for a well-paid job.'

# CHAPTER 3
## *A High Hum of Pure Agony*

A script direction for *Under the Loofah Tree*.
Giles Cooper 1958.

'A high hum of pure agony' was one of Giles Cooper's sound requirements for the radio play *Under the Loofah Tree* which was made in 1958 and consolidated the techniques used in *The Disagreeable Oyster*.

*Under the Loofah Tree* was written specifically for the Radiophonic Workshop. It was an immediate tribute to the newly-born department, and the production – a radio classic – was a precursor of the many distinguished, extraordinary and experimental programmes that would subsequently bear the credit: 'Realised at the Radiophonic Workshop'.

*Under the Loofah Tree*, described by Desmond Briscoe as 'a sort of *This Is Your Life* in the bath', tells of Edward Thwaite, a king in his bath water, oblivious to the world around him. Outside the door his wife despairs, his son cries at the key-hole, a travelling salesman and a man with a summons stand in wait. But for Edward Thwaite the whole world – for the moment – is the bathroom, and through it pass, Walter-Mitty-like, fact and fantasy, the as-it-was and the might-have-been.

Giles Cooper wrote: 'Part of the attraction of writing for radio lies in the fact that for no other medium can one write pieces like this which are neither fact nor fiction, neither prose nor poetry, and which have no being except on the air.'

When it was first broadcast, *Under the Loofah Tree* received enormous critical and popular acclaim. Desmond Briscoe's later production in stereo stuck firmly to the original concept and introduced a modern audience to a classic radio play.

Nearly fifty programme commitments were completed in the first year, 1958, starting before the Workshop opened with *Amphitryon 38*, a television comedy starring Googie Withers and Alec Clunes. The radiophonic elements in this production were amongst the earliest of any for BBC television. Cast and critics alike were excited by Daphne Oram's music.

Donald McWhinnie's radio production of James Hanley's *The Ocean*, another early programme employing radiophonic treatment, received something of a hammering for its special sounds from the *Sunday Times*, whose critic commented that they dislocated the harmony of the play and were conceived 'in a wilfully fantastic vein'.

Desmond Briscoe's brief had been to create a sound that would suggest the monotony of the scene confronting five men adrift in an open boat with heavy swell and a never-changing horizon of sea and sky. To the *Sunday Times* critic, the 'ghostly trumpeting' sounded more like the noise of 'elephants in a claustrophobic forest, perhaps; certainly not whales at sea'. Having subsequently heard genuine recordings of the hump-backed whale, Desmond Briscoe reckons with hindsight that by chance his sounds were very close to the real thing.

As the Workshop went about its business of providing radiophonic music and sound for television and radio, a group of BBC delegates visited the 'Journées Internationales de Musique Expérimentale' in Brussels in October 1958, an event which, for some of them, was not a total success. When they returned, their reports talked of lack of mutual understanding, bad organisation, tape machines constantly breaking down, and compositions which were much too loud and noisy.

'It may be,' wrote E.W.S. ('Pip') Porter, Assistant Head of Central Programme Operations, 'that if this movement gathers momentum, the BBC will be forced eventually to participate, employing composers. Should this happen, I submit that an additional workshop will be essential, for such composition takes a very long time and inevitably a competent studio manager will have to do the job with the composer replacing a producer. Stockhausen is alleged to have spent six months producing fifteen minutes of programme.

'I left Brussels fully convinced that the way the Corporation develops and uses radiophonic effects is the right way. *Vive Le Workshop!*'

Not every delegate felt quite the same way. Daphne Oram had for long been exploring the world of experimental music. She had submitted to the BBC, as far back as 1950, a work for 'orchestra, five microphones, and manipulated recordings' and she returned from Brussels determined to continue in this field of music. The Workshop, though busier than ever, was busy about 'sound' rather than music. In January 1959, after fifteen years with the BBC, she resigned, withdrew her pension money and used it to set up her own studio in a Kentish oast house. This became the setting for Daphne's experiments into 'Oramics', for which she subsequently received two Gulbenkian Foundation Grants.

Since then she has become internationally known for her work in films, television and theatre; presented successful concerts of electronic

*Right*: Daphne Oram in 1958 with wobbulator recording on the Reflectograph, one of the earliest speed change machines

compositions at the Mermaid Theatre, London, and at the Edinburgh Festival, and lectured widely – at London University, Cambridge University Arts Society, The Institute of Physics, Harrow School, Wellington College, Roedean and at many other colleges, schools and music festivals.

About the time that Daphne Oram, the senior founder member of the Workshop, relinquished her position, the others were creating the sounds for *Quatermass and the Pit*, one of the first really big television productions undertaken by the unit, and important in that it was the first television programme to hit a wide audience with strange and weird radiophonic sound.

One of the great television directors of all time, Rudolph Cartier, directed the production and he and the author, Nigel Kneale, discussed their requirements at some length, since sound was of paramount importance in the story. Desmond Briscoe says:

We made great electronic churnings and throbbings for the sequence in which they dig down and find the buried spaceship. For these sounds we used tape feed-back started with a side-drum beat, and tape-recorders that went into oscillation with themselves. We also connected and disconnected amplifiers to make great splats of sound. Finally we transferred all the sound that we had made onto discs to play in the television studios.

*Quatermass and the Pit* fully justified the Workshop's late-night sessions fulfilling the script requirements for 'Droning pulse, into bell and into deep vibration' . . . 'Quick "glunks" with build-up' . . . 'Giant electrical discharge' . . . 'Electronic vibration with occult noises' . . . 'Martian crowd chatter'. . . . Not only did the television audience sit up and take notice, but many more television makers came to Maida Vale to find out how the unit could play a part in their own productions.

Desmond Briscoe: From then on it developed very quickly in terms of programme demand. The programme producers who came to see us may not have been very impressed by the equipment we had, but they liked what we were doing.

Freddy Bradnum, author of *Private Dreams and Public Nightmares*, was, about this time, fearful that television encroachment would swamp the Workshop's resources. His fears proved to be without substance, although, as he commented later:

I suspect that the Workshop was only saved by the discovery that radiophonic sound was an extremely useful addition to television programmes as well as radio. I think that if they had been making sounds for radio only the whole thing may never have gone beyond a little backroom studio.

Desmond Briscoe says: In its second year, the infant Workshop struggled for life, not entirely helped by the fact that its 'nursemaids' (the creative staff) were changed regularly, due to a belief that there was a very real danger 'the lunatic fringe' might take over and the place develop an uncontrollable life of its own. The noisy offspring was also restricted to a very meagre diet of facilities and equipment, but there was certainly no shortage of programme commitments or ideas.

Management thought that if any one person worked on radiophonic music and sound for more than three months, they would go mad. Maybe we did! But the consequence of people continually coming and going was that they worked their way from A to C, and then the next person started at A again. Since there was no possibility of passing on techniques, or developing a collective experience, we didn't progress as far as we might have done.

Nevertheless, the Workshop had a busy and eventful year and in April was given the go-ahead for an improvement scheme with radio and television contributing to the costs on a 60/40 basis.

Output almost doubled, and the Workshop began to export its sounds abroad, ironically to Germany, where the Cologne Studios had played a seminal role in the generation of electronic music. When the BBC was planning its stand at the prestigious Berlin Fair, it invited the Maida Vale unit to provide a continuous background of radiophonic sound. The Workshop was proud to oblige, and from this time onwards there was an increasing European awareness that the BBC was now seriously in the business of manipulating sounds.

At about the same time, followers of *The Goon Show* sat up and took notice as the Workshop provided an unforgettable contribution: Major Bloodnok's stomach. The Workshop's first version was thirty seconds long – doing full justice to the gastric disorders of a military character with a taste for strong curry and ladies of easy virtue. It wasn't so much a performance as a symphony, with as many funny sounds as could be pieced together in a montage of inner plumbing. Dick Mills and Jimmy Burnett compounded a mixture of burps, whoops from oscillators, water splashes and cork-like pops until they had constructed something that sounded great but was far too long and would have stopped the show dead.

Dick Mills remembers: 'We hacked it down with razor-blades and sticky tape until finally it was down to twelve seconds, just right for the fast-moving Goons humour.' Major Bloodnok's exploding stomach can be heard today on the Workshop's Twenty-first Birthday LP and is a classic of its kind, quite different from the nightmares and space odysseys usually associated with the unit.

Shortly afterwards, *The Goon Show* came up with another request: could the Workshop please provide the right sounds for the ascent of a rice-paper balloon? Though the Maida Vale unit could – and did – there was a disquieting feeling behind the scenes that once Mr Sellers and Mr Milligan had discovered the place and what it could do, that would be the end of civilisation as it had previously been known. The threatened collapse never happened: most probably because the Goons had already established their own style of expertly put together sound effects.

Not that that was entirely that, as an exchange of letters between Spike Milligan and Desmond Briscoe in *The Listener* was ten years later to reveal:

### Goon Sounds

Sir: Reading *The Listener*, 18 December 1969 (I really must get a new newsagent), I note Michael Mason's reference to the unique oral surrealism of *The Goon Show*. I must add that this was only part of the development. It was audio sound effects, and their use of time, that really made it work. For instance, the agony of getting the sound of a Wurlitzer organ driving down the street, changing gear into a different key (I think top gear was C sharp above the stave), and then progressing, getting faster, which meant that the music not only had to be chromatic, but also broken down into quarter tones, and eighth tones, 16th tones and 32nd tones, and so on until it was crescendo. What in fact finally made me pack in the show was the inability to get the then newly-formed Radiophonic Workshop, who serviced all the shows, using electronics. If I had been given that service, the show might have gone on another two series, but at the time we had exhausted every possible computation of sound effects that the BBC had.

I am full of all the useless type of information. Write now for full details.     SPIKE MILLIGAN

London W2.
(April 1970 *Listener*)

### Goon Sounds

Sir: Whilst I would be the first to acknowledge the debt we all owe to the *Goon Show* for pioneering the truly imaginative use of sound, I well remember the long – and involved – telephone conversation I had with Spike Milligan, when I declined to allow the Radiophonic Workshop to become exclusively the *Goon Show* Sound-Shop. The Workshop has serviced all programmes, including the Goons, and 'Major Bloodnok's Stomach' is surely a classic example of early Radiophonic composition. To stand accused ten years later (*Listener*, 30 April) of being virtually responsible for the premature demise of *The Goons* is indeed a heavy burden, lightened a little by the fact that the Radiophonic Workshop has survived, to be part of Broadcasting in the Seventies.

Radiophonic Workshop, BBC     DESMOND BRISCOE
(May 1970 *Listener*)

The year 1961's most ambitious collaboration was with anglicised Spanish composer Roberto Gerhard, which culminated in Dick Mills supporting live performances of Gerhard's work at both the Royal Albert Hall and also the Royal Festival Hall under the baton of Rudolph Schwartz.

This came about through an earlier collaboration between the Workshop and Gerhard on *Asylum Diary* – a title which indicates the programme's suitability for radiophonic treatment. Gerhard came to Maida Vale and after watching Desmond Briscoe working with tape remarked that his 'whole stance and attitude while working was that of a blind man'.

Later, when Desmond Briscoe complimented the composer on the strange and completely random cracking sounds which provided a tension-heightening element within the music, Gerhard – whom the Workshop staff always referred to affectionately as 'Britain's oldest young composer' – smiled a slow-spreading smile and replied, 'That was the log fire crackling as I was recording in the sitting room. Never rule out chance,' he added.

Gerhard returned to the unit to ask for assistance with Lorca's poem 'Lament for the Death of a Bullfighter', a reading of the poem set to Gerhard's own radiophonic music.

The BBC then commissioned Gerhard to write a concert work, which he called *Collages*, in which the manipulated sound was introduced into traditional orchestral textures. The work was extremely serious in intent, and generally well received by the critics. In the spirit of the collage technique, pre-recorded tape-sounds and orchestral passages were mixed and matched, sometimes in conflict, sometimes in relaxation. Some music lovers, however, found it ahead of its time, as was to be proved at the public concert at the Royal Festival Hall.

> Dick Mills comments: 'Roberto had a rather difficult problem to overcome when attempting to record his basic sounds, as he lived on a busy trunk road in Cambridgeshire and the only quiet period was around 3.30 in the morning. One can imagine the scene as Roberto twanged and banged and bonked metallic objects as his wife Poldi acted as recording engineer. Both of them were in their sixties at the time.'

Gerhard brought the basic sound material to the Workshop where it was mixed and prepared and made ready for playing with the orchestral parts. As Dick was familiar with it, it was decided that he should perform with the orchestra.

> Dick Mills: We had a rehearsal with the BBC Symphony Orchestra under Rudolf Schwartz, and the tape was switched on at just the right place in the score for the first tape-recorded 'solo'. After the bangs, twangs and plonks had gone on for a while, the back row of the fiddles started tittering a bit, and this became infectious until the whole orchestra dissolved in a polite sort of controlled mirth. The conductor turned to Gerhard and apologised: 'I'm sorry, but it's the first time we've ever heard anything like it. How can you forgive us?' We performed *Collages* first at the Royal Festival Hall.

There were four loudspeakers in the orchestra so that the tape sound would be heard from there, and we were up in the boxes behind the conductor with two tape machines which ran simultaneously in case of breakdown; a studio manager who was turning the score and controlling the volume, and an announcer – all of us wearing dinner jackets though the audience couldn't see us, or even suspect that we were there.

At the end of any modern work there's always that period of uncertainty when the audience is not sure whether it has finished or not, and in the micro-second between the chords finally dying away and the first clap starting, somebody managed to shout out 'Rubbish'. We were never sure whether the applause that followed was for the piece or for the person who shouted out 'rubbish'.

Subsequently we did another performance at the Proms in the Albert Hall and I was on the stage this time under the beady eye of Sir Henry Wood's bust. We're not sure that he would have approved at all, but none of us were struck down by a thunderbolt baton from heaven and everything went quite well.

A loop being set up on the variable speed tape-recorder

Having been featured previously in Berlin, the Workshop unveiled itself in 1962 to the great British public at the Radio Show at Earls Court, London. It was, in its way, a return from the high art endeavour of European concrete and electronic music to the music hall. Desmond Briscoe and Dick Mills, for the good of the cause, duly appeared under the billing 'Weird and Wonderful' in live performance (between the Eric Delaney Big Band and Johnny Morris's 'Animal Magic') in a BBC Show at Earls Court which represented the work of the Maida Vale unit, now four years old.

To this day neither man is sure who was 'Weird' and who 'Wonderful', but the double-act worked well. The passing public were enthralled by the sound of Desmond Briscoe hitting a row of bottles and turning the sound into rhythm by means of tape manipulation. Having established the rhythm, out of the wings sprang the Malcolm Mitchell Trio playing the 'front' to the bottle backing. To Earls Court visitors it was obvious that the BBC Radiophonic Workshop was alive and well and continuing to amaze in live performance as well as on radio and television.

# CHAPTER 4
## *Glowpot Days*

'The story of the Radiophonic Workshop and its machines is
really the story of people opening the backs of those
machines and doing things they weren't meant to do'
*Brian Hodgson, Organiser, Radiophonic Workshop*

The Radiophonic Workshop's first year witnessed the enthusiasts, still
enthusiastic, hard at work in a cave-like room full of largely redundant
equipment, and with the rather ominous address of Room 13, Maida
Vale. Despite the comings and goings of staff 'resting' from 'battle
fatigue', the year ended satisfactorily in that the demand for
radiophonic sound had steadily increased throughout the year and
there was no doubt that the experiment had proved a success.

Though the staple fare of the unit had been primarily radio drama –
only to be expected since that was how the Workshop had started in the
first place – the year began and ended with important television
productions that introduced a new and larger popular audience to
radiophonic sound.

Working conditions were far from perfect. The studio's ventilator fan
let in so much unwanted noise that staff were driven to stuff rags into it
and suffer as long as they could until the place became unbearably hot.
The rags were then taken out, the room vacated, the place aired, and
later they all trooped back again.

Throughout 1959 BBC Management had been applying itself to the
future of the Workshop in terms of equipment, accommodation and,
most important of all, its staff.

By March 1960 they had made their decision – and Desmond Briscoe
was appointed permanently to manage the 'Radiophonic Workshop'.

His report at that time took stock of the Workshop's present position,
assessed its achievements, and looked towards a plan for the future. The
tardy arrival of much-needed new equipment was contrasted with the
speedier build-up of television demand. The proportion of television to
radio commitments was sometimes 80%/20% in favour of television in
one month, and it never fell below 60%/40%.

Fortunately, continued the report, we now have a very competent
staff to cope with this demand. To date, the achievements and
success of the Workshop has been considerable, often in spite of the

lack or inadequacy of the equipment and facilities provided; new techniques have been developed and old ones consolidated, quality has improved, man-hours per commitment have decreased, partly because of the new equipment we already have, but principally because we have reached a professional standard of approach and execution.

The appointment of Desmond Briscoe to direct and develop the Radiophonic Workshop gave it a sense of purpose and identity, plus the will to undertake commitments of ever-increasing variety and complexity. From now on the credit 'Sound and music by the Radiophonic Workshop' became increasingly familiar, and there was a growing demand for Desmond Briscoe to give public lectures to schools, colleges, universities, learned societies, and associations and social gatherings of every description. Desmond Briscoe believes that any success that the Workshop has had may be directly attributed to the fact that no 'technician' is ever allowed to come between the composer and his music.

The Radiophonic Workshop is perhaps unique among electronic

Room 13 at the Radiophonic Workshop in 1974

music studios in that the composing staff are their own 'operators', and indeed the operational techniques have always been regarded as part of the creative process.

When BBC Television Centre opened in 1960, one of the changes to mark the event was new music to replace the Eric Coates Television March which had, since Alexandra Palace days, provided a two-minute run-up to allow viewers to adjust their sets before the programmes began.

When viewers tuned in to see and hear the Two O'clock Television News they were more than surprised by what they heard. Whilst there was still an echo of Eric Coates' theme, Desmond Briscoe had realised his march electronically at the Workshop in a way which some viewers appreciated, and others did not!

*The Radio Times 24.11.60*

**Orwellian?**

Please use your influence to stop that dreadful introduction to BBC-TV programmes which shows what appears to be the various departments of an Orwellian prison.

Or does the background music intend it should be taken for a lunatic asylum? – (Lt-Col) R.K. Spurrell, Leigh, Surrey.

*The Radio Times 8.12.60*

**Prelude to BBC-TV**

I entirely disagree with Lt-Col. R.K. Spurrell (Radio Times, Nov 24). The introduction to BBC-TV is an excellent idea, and what is more it is unusual, and something the other channel hasn't got. As for the music suggesting a lunatic asylum, I think it is wonderful, and would like to know if it is possible to get the record. – Katherina M. Cooper (14), Wollaton, Nottingham.

(Sorry, no, this is BBC Radiophonic Workshop music – Editor)

*The Radio Times 10.11.60*

**From the Workshop**

What is the noise supposed to be that precedes the two-o'clock Television News? It sounds like a nightmare in a railway train! – F.M.M., Shrewsbury.

(This is BBC Radiophonic Workshop music, based on the theme of the specially commissioned march by Eric Coates which for many years was heard opening the BBC Television Service.

This introductory routine, together with the fascinating camera shots of the TV Centre, provides a signal for making final adjustments during the period when viewers are normally warming up their receivers before programmes begin.)

As one radio critic put it: 'Now that radiophonics have broken out, only heaven knows what to expect!'

Since the Workshop's equipment was still extremely basic, Maida Vale in the early 1960s was a place where ingenuity ruled, rather than the rule book. Very little equipment could be bought tailor-made to fulfil the Workshop's needs. What was available was adapted to its new use and given an appropriate name. A mixing desk which faded sounds up and down without unwanted wave-form clicks was operated through little light-sensitive transistors and glowing lightbulbs. It was called 'The Glowpot Desk'.

A quarter of a century has seen much ingenuity and development of a similar nature, and the galloping technology of recent years has speeded up the process. 'The Glowpot Desk' has given way to the world's most advanced computer musical instrument which creates a keyboard of sound from drawings done with a light-pen.

The Glowpot Desk incorporating the crackle-free light-operated faders devised by Dave Young who succeeded 'Dickie' Bird as engineer for the Radiophonic Workshop

Dave Young

The late Richard 'Dickie' Bird was the Workshop's first resident engineer, working at Maida Vale from the Workshop's inception until 1963, when he died. In one room, 'Dickie' presided over some rather nondescript secondhand equipment that included a beat frequency oscillator known popularly as the 'wobbulator' and the first pair of professional tape machines owned by the BBC. The mixing desk had actually been used in the Albert Hall during the war.

'The Workshop was a very Heath Robinson set-up when I arrived,' says David Young, who was the Workshop's next engineer in residence. David commuted to London from his home at Havant, near Portsmouth, but still arrived early enough to call in at Portobello Road before work every Friday morning.

It was just as well that he did, for his capacity for making things from other people's cast-offs and junk was to become legendary and would provide the Workshop with much-needed equipment that would not have been obtainable in any other way.

David used components he came across on the Havant rubbish-tip and in the Portobello Road, London's long-established fleamarket where anything and everything is for sale at a price.

'I had the freedom to tinker about at something I enjoyed doing, and to make things that wouldn't otherwise have been made available for people to use creatively,' says David, from a happy retirement still filled with 'tinkering'. His maxim was that if he could understand what was required, then he could eventually make it out of other people's junk.

Desmond Briscoe: Rumour has it that the BBC Appointments Board that interviewed David for the Workshop job were enormously impressed that he had a house full of Hammond Organs that he had built himself. As the Hammond Organ was in those days the nearest thing to a synthesiser (which had yet to be invented) the Board nodded its collective head sagely and gave him the job.

David really was a most remarkable chap who, during the war, had the misfortune to be captured and imprisoned by the Germans. But he put his POW incarceration to good use by helping make radio sets out of nothing so that he and his fellow POWs could hear the BBC News Service. He would then disguise the sets as accordions or gramophones. He was never found out. If he had been rumbled, then in all probability he would never have made it to Maida Vale.

David Young was the man who struggled to Maida Vale one day with the Workshop's largest musical instrument to date: a Victorian harmonium. Later the Workshop was to acquire a second and even more magnificent harmonium – this time a Canadian instrument built in 1887, the pedals of which bore the inscription: MOUSE-PROOF PEDALS!

The Heath Robinson charm of the early days was great fun while it lasted. Bottles could be chinkled, blown across or rolled on surfaces and recorded. Other 'concrete' sounds came from whatever was to hand. These basic sounds were eventually made into music by contraptions of the most elaborate ingenuity, as Desmond Briscoe recollects:

> One of David's devices was for creating a chorus of sounds. It was a Hammond Organ-type affair which ran off an old gramophone motor which David had found in Portobello Road. Since David liked to case his equipment handsomely, the Chorus Unit was at first housed in a 1930s' art-deco radio cabinet. It was such a useful piece of equipment that I asked him to make us another. When we couldn't find a matching case he used Perspex instead so that we could see what was going on inside. It became known as The Crystal Palace, and the original one was re-cased accordingly. They still exist at the Workshop, though we don't use them nowadays.

The Crystal Palace

One of David Young's most useful inventions was a spring-loaded loopstand for supporting loops of recording tape. When David complained that producers were always 'fiddling with them and breaking them', his assistant at the time inscribed each such device with the legend: DO NOT FIDDLE WITH, and it is by this name that they are known today.

*Above:* Dave Young's invention for supporting loops of tape

*Left:* Concrete sound can be made from bottles, bells, musical instruments, cans, tin drums . . .

David's remote-start switches for tape machines were made from the small metal tins that pick-up heads came in. The tip of a Conway-Stewart fountain pen played an important part in one piece of equipment as an output contact.

His Keying Unit described by present-day engineer Ray White as 'a sort of primitive synthesiser where you had to tweak each note', was a bank of twelve conventional oscillators, normally used to test equipment, but now connected to a keyboard which 'gated' the sound, turning it on and off at a prescribed rate, thus providing an 'attack' and 'decay' to each note.

When David finally retired, he was threatened with one of his own Crystal Palaces as a leaving gift. But he demurred. Instead, the Workshop presented him with 'a beautiful old brass and copper loudspeaker – the sort of thing that he might have found in Portobello Road on a particularly good day'.

Brian Hodgson, who joined the Workshop in 1963 and became its Organiser in 1977, remembers the original Motosacoche tape-recorders:

The famous Motosacoche tape-recorders, some of the earliest tape-recorders bought by the BBC. They took fifteen seconds to get up to speed

Although they took fifteen seconds to come up to speed, once they were there these two monolithic things would stay in synchronisation all day long. Which was more than you could say for a lot of tape-recorders, until quite recently.

The main reason that we got rid of them was that they took up so much room. The deckplate was one-and-a-half inches of steel, and instead of the tape being pulled away from the heads, the heads were pulled away from the tape. When anything went wrong, we would press the button and the decks of these giant machines would gradually go up in the air; we would put in four safety pegs, and walk underneath with a spanner and adjust them. Just like servicing a car.

Making sounds took a very long time in those days. The copying process involved in making concrete music built up a tremendous amount of hiss, and we had to keep putting 'top cut' on to such an extent that the Workshop had the reputation of never producing anything above middle C!

In 1961 there were two studios in operation which made things much easier. By 1962, when we had taken delivery of six Philips tape-recorders, we could cut down the hiss and kill the 'middle C' legend dead, since we could now reproduce high frequencies and did not have to filter them out with the hiss.

The new machines enabled Delia Derbyshire, who had by then joined the Workshop, to realise the first hi-fi signature tune; for the Arabic Service 'Science and Industry' programme. It was at the time when the Arabs were realising the importance of their oil, and the BBC wanted to have a special signature tune for this programme, rather than the usual theme – which was also a Workshop product made by Phil Young in 1959 and used for other programmes in the Science and Industry series. Delia came up with a chugalug oilwell sound that is featured – with other pieces of the period – on the LP *Radiophonic Workshop – 21*.

Though the tune actually lasts only 22 seconds, the mechanics of making such a piece were long and involved. Once a sound was chosen it was tuned, cut out, cut again to the right length, duplicated, and joined together with the previous note, and so on, until each line of the music was prepared and ready to be played in synchronisation.

The loops of tape used in any composition could be of any length. Some were tiny, and some very long indeed. Though the story of one loop going all the way round the room and out of the door and down the corridor as far as the commissionaire's desk at Maida Vale entrance hall, and then back again, may be exaggerated, Brian Hodgson remembers one that went round the 25 feet long by 18 feet wide Room 13.

At that time the Workshop did not possess any loop stands, and so the recording tape was passed round milk bottles filled with water to weight them down. Brian was taking some Japanese visitors around the Workshop one day when one of the party said: 'What is this, please?', and took hold of the loop. 'As the loop tightened,' says Brian, 'everything shot in all directions and there were milk bottles flying around, water everywhere and utter confusion. Naturally, the piece was ruined and we had to start again. "Madam," I replied, "That *was* a tape loop".'

Though the BBC was now willing to fund the unit more generously than in the past, this didn't mean that it was providing an open cheque. Everything that the unit needed had to be provenly useful and accounted for to the last detail.

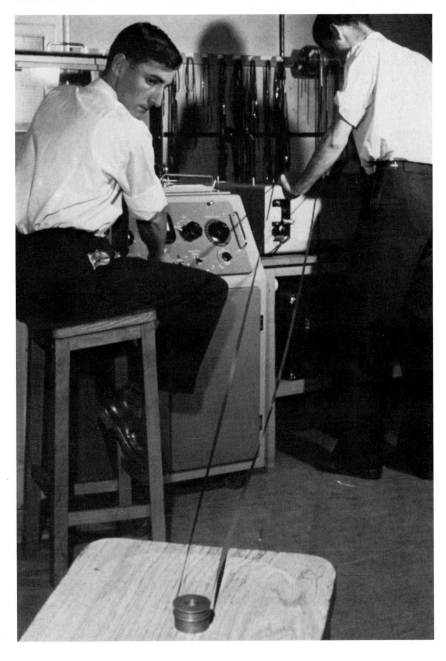

Dick Mills (left) and John Harrison playing a tape loop. Dozens more loops hang on the hooks on the wall

A memo from Desmond Briscoe requested permission to purchase drumsticks and beaters required 'for playing the various percussion instruments owned by staff and for use on BBC percussion instruments in studios. We also require hard and medium rubber sticks for our recent acquisition, the "percussion hammerless piano".' This elegant-sounding instrument was actually the guts of an elderly piano which was later to find fame as the sound source for Doctor Who's space/time ship, The Tardis. Another of Desmond's claims for petty-cash reimbursement was for a miniature zither: 'a small melodic instrument very rich in harmonics and an excellent sound source of a quality that cannot be got from the guitar or piano. Whilst on holiday I saw such a zither in a second-hand shop in Oxford, and having tried it and been satisfied that it would suit our purpose, and after some bargaining, I bought it for £2.10s. I trust this can be met out of the usual fund.'

Both memos met with eventual approval, and the new acquisitions joined a motley collection which included Desmond Briscoe's own drum kit, an Arabian double-reed pipe called a Mijwiz, a child's tin xylophone, a Melodica (a key-operated mouth-organ known variously in the Workshop as a 'one-stringed harmonica' or an 'edible piano'), a home-made electric guitar and a BBC green lampshade that Delia Derbyshire made peculiarly her own.

Fortunately, together with such unsophisticated equipment and musical aids, went a lot of imagination, effort and ambition so that the Workshop was able to survive and thrive over twenty years and eventually emerge into a quite different age – that of the Computer Musical Instrument.

Thus was fulfilled a visionary description by Francis Bacon, who in 1624 wrote about the Sound-houses of the New Atlantis. . . .

*Left:* Desmond Briscoe with what remains of his original drum kit
*Inset:* Desmond Briscoe and the Mijwiz

*Right:* Fantasy for three Crystal Palaces (left) two Jasons (centre top) and an Albis (bottom right)

# CHAPTER 5
## *The New Atlantis*

'Wee have also Sound-houses, wher wee practise and demonstrate all Sounds, and their Generation. Wee have Harmonies which you have not, of Quarter-Sounds, and lesser Slides of Sounds. Diverse Instruments of Musick likewise to you unknowne, some sweeter then any you have; Together with Bells and Rings that are dainty and sweet. Wee represent Small Sounds as Great and Deepe; Likeweise Great Sounds, Extenuate and Sharpe; Wee make diverse Tremblings and Warblings of Sounds, which in their Originall are Entire. Wee represent and imitate all Articulate Sounds and Letters, and the Voices and Notes of Beasts and Birds. Wee have certaine Helps, which sett to the Eare doe further the Hearing greatly. Wee have also diverse Strange and Artificiall Eccho's, Reflecting the Voice many times, and as it were Tossing it: And some that give back the Voice Lowder then it come, some Shriller, and some Deeper; Yea some rendring the Voice, Differing in the Letters or Articulate Sound, from that they receyve, Wee have also meanes to convey Sounds in Trunks and Pipes, in strange Lines, and Distances.'

*Extract from* The New Atlantis *by Francis Bacon, 1624*

At the 'New Atlantis' in Maida Vale in the autumn of 1982 the new studio A contained only a Mixing Desk and the smell of new paint.

The desk alone had cost something in the region of £16,000, and the studio itself was about to receive its new occupant. Whilst the Workshop's engineers, Ray White and Ray Riley, had been labouring away on their sixth complete rebuild in four years, this particular Workshop composer had been away having a baby.

When Elizabeth Parker returned, her studio was brand spanking new, all set for a twelve-month involvement with David Attenborough's next major BBC TV series *Living Planet*. Looking something like a larger version of the Concorde's cockpit, Studio A now contains some £60,000 worth of ultra-modern electronic equipment.

In the centre of everything is the dominant control centre, the Mixing Desk, winking and blinking its little red and green lights in a bewildering array of hundreds of buttons, switches, knobs, dials and faders. The desk takes inputs from tape machines, microphones and synthesisers; digests and passes them out through all the various treatment devices and back again via a multi-track recorder to the control centre from whence the sound and music finally return to single quarter-inch tape to be married with radio and television programmes.

*Top right:* Ray White, Engineer, Radiophonic Workshop

*Bottom right:* Ray Riley, Engineer, Radiophonic Workshop, drilling a component for the installation of Studio A

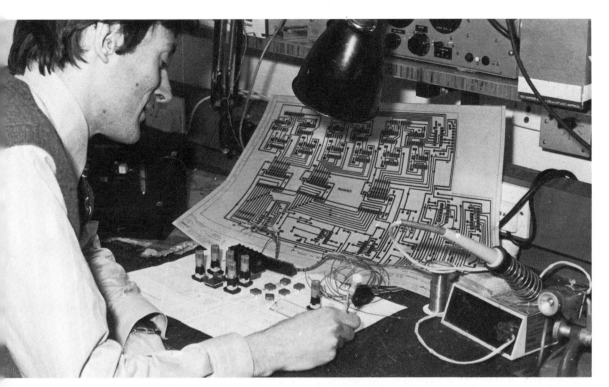

On the wall are three telephones connected to the Workshop's 'front office': red-green-outgoing. No one can bother the composer unless he or she wants to be bothered. Understanding secretaries listen to 'work-in-progress' on the intercom and if the composer is in the middle of a piece will ask the caller to try again later.

Studio A has much in common with the other Workshop studios. Though individual composers will personalise their studios in their own way, the basic equipment remains constant: mixing desk . . . sub mixer . . . synthesisers . . . treatment equipment . . . multitrack tape-recorder . . . $\frac{1}{4}$-inch tape-recorders. . . noise reduction. . . speakers. . . echo device . . . video. . . .

In order to reach Studio A, the visitor comes off the street into a bustling entrance hall which is frequently full of musicians, instrument cases, and chatter.

The original foyer of the Skating Palace is now hung with huge photographs of classical musicians, composers and conductors. There are deep armchairs about, usually occupied. The commissionaire's phones ring continuously. The BBC Symphony Orchestra has 101 members and the Radio Orchestra 56; together with soloists and chorus there could easily be two hundred or more people passing through at busy times.

Elizabeth Parker in her original studio, Studio H, in 1982. She i adjusting the equalisation of the synthesiser

54

But take a sharp turn left at street level, through several sets of doors, and all is quiet again. Along what is reputed to be the longest corridor in the entire BBC, the Radiophonic Workshop keeps a low profile, the biggest clue being the sounds that emanate from behind closed doors. Otherwise, only discreet doorplates tell you that you are now deep in radiophonic territory.

The corridor's curiously neutral atmosphere, where people pass by with abstracted faces, reminds the visitor of the placid swan: serenely sailing above water but paddling like hell beneath the surface.

Blue 'studio-in-operation' lights indicate activity: open any door of the ten studios (six for individual composers, the other four for viewing, recording musicians or actors or screening television films on Steenbeck machines), and the nature of that activity becomes apparent.

Journalists have written about the 'walls of unimposing grey', and of walking 'down long corridors through swing doors which seem to mark the End of the World As We Know It' and have said that it is all 'very unobtrusive, one suspects so as not to disturb the natives'.

But then, journalists do tend to go overboard when describing the Workshop and its occupants. Desmond Briscoe's forehead was once described in print as 'a domed electronic orb which, one fancies, glows as he talks'. Actually, it doesn't, and he is an essentially practical man equally interested in boats and boating as in poetry and synthesisers. The composers of radiophonic music and sound are not white-overalled but ordinarily dressed in jeans and pullovers or smart sports gear. Sober suits are only worn on special occasions, and ties are not *de rigueur*. Only the Workshop's Organiser, Brian Hodgson, cuts a romantically weird figure as he disappears into the Maida Vale night in an Andy Pandy boiler-suit, with light-reflecting yellow braces and a reversible peaked cap. But then, Brian goes home by bike.

Apart from Desmond Briscoe, Brian Hodgson and their 'front office' staff, a visitor is unlikely to find the composer he wants at home, unless he has taken the precaution of phoning first. Being completely self-scheduling, the composers come and go as and when they choose to a Workshop that never closes.

Some are larks and some, owls. Every one of them works alone whilst composing and realising their music, but before, during and after every commitment will be heavily involved with the production team wherever they may be working. So there is a continuous traffic between Maida Vale, Broadcasting House and Television Centre.

A home base much used for programme discussions is the Maida Vale canteen – always providing a 200-strong contingent of orchestral players are not having their coffee break at the same time.

The further you progress into the Workshop area, the more information you find on the doors. Studio D has the added letters 'ICK', just to make clear to everyone that Dick Mills lives there. Pictures of The Tardis and the various Doctors Who decorate the door.

Similarly, Studio C has 'LARKE' appended – not because Malcolm Clarke gets in early in the morning but just to show who lives here. Since his of all the Workshop's studios most resembles an art student's bed-sit, it would not be difficult to recognise even without the stickers on the door supporting wild-life and Percy Grainger!

Behind many of the doors, late in the evening, the sounds still continue. . . . Some of them being made, perhaps, on a machine called the Fairlight Computer Musical Instrument, one of the Workshop's most powerful allies to date. Long past are the 'Glowpot Days' of do-it-yourself equipment. Synthesisers are standard aids and have done away with much of the drudgery of realisation. The Fairlight offers an almost alchemical combination of concrete music and electronic music all available in the one piece of equipment.

Malcolm Clarke demonstrating not only his manual dexterity but also the cramped conditions of Studio C

Peter Howell didn't wait long before finding out what it could do. 'More in anger than intent I banged the side of a new mixer. It had a beautiful ring to it, so I sampled it on the Fairlight and worked up a pleasing little piece.'

Desmond Briscoe: In the past, electronic sound has tended to be dehumanised, and boring, because it was created from very basic waveforms. Natural sounds have much more information in them. They are warmer and more interesting than synthesised sounds; using the Fairlight's ability to provide the composer with a means of *playing* real sounds is a return to the early days without all the disadvantages of tape manipulation. Even with electronic sounds it is possible to build in arbitrary variations to approximate more closely to the kind of accidental imperfections of acoustic instruments and their performance which makes them so enjoyable, and so beautiful.

eter Howell demonstrating the
airlight Computer Musical
strument shortly after its
urchase in 1981

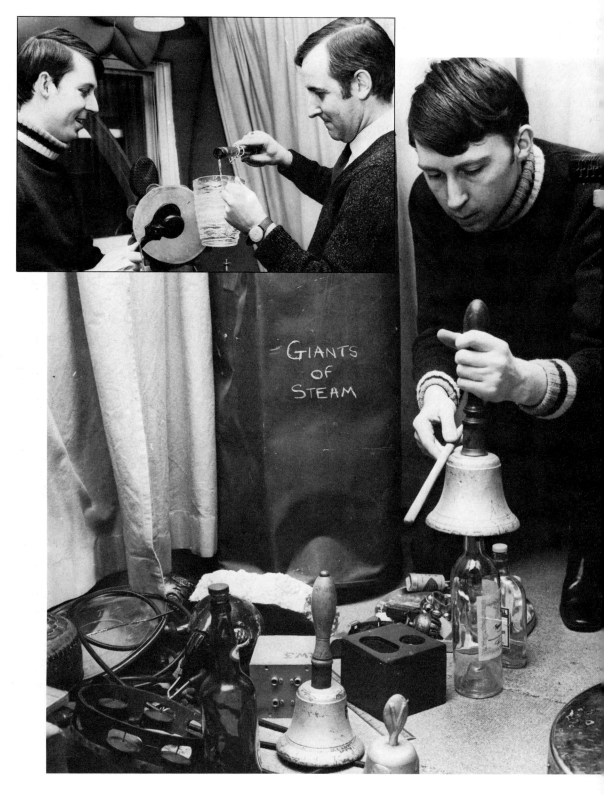

*t: Musique Concrète* was still
ve and well at the Workshop
the 'seventies as demonstrated
Malcolm Clarke
*et:* Tied up in the background
ickly green foam which was
ing used, experimentally, as
oustic treatment

Brian Hodgson welcomes *musique concrète* back like an old friend.

For all its amazing virtues, the Fairlight just brings us back the natural sounds that have been missing from our work in recent years.

Roger Limb set about using the Fairlight recently to illustrate in sound 'a lot of little germs eating away at plaque surrounding the teeth'.

I scrunched an apple and put it on tape, then fed it into the Fairlight and started playing it on the keyboard. It worked very well as an effect. There was a sound there that *could* be arranged in a musical fashion – which brings up the great big important question to which all of us reply 'Goodness knows!'

The question: 'When is a sound a sound, and music music?' In other words, where is the borderline between sound and music?

As to the future, Brian Hodgson hopes that the Workshop will come to be considered differently by programme producers.

Much more as an ingredient of the cake rather than just the icing on top. Instead of coming along rather late in the day when he's probably done a whole lot of things that make our job more difficult, he will consider using us right at the start and discussing with us the direction in which we will all be going.

Peter Howell believes that the Workshop is entering a new Golden Age:

BBC Graphics Department are producing pictures by video synthesisers and computers and very soon TV producers will become enthusiastic about linking that with what we are doing at Maida Vale. Who knows, we might bring back the TV interludes between programmes that we used to have years ago, but with all-electronic pictures and sounds instead of strings and floating swans. Pop videos have shown the way and we could make amazing music to stunning visual effects in a series of images to evoke any emotion.

Malcolm Clarke agrees: 'We are looking towards not just a Radiophonic Workshop but a Telephonic Workshop, where the aural and visual elements are much more closely wedded. I don't mean that we should become part of television, but that we should work much more closely with visuals so that we complement them perfectly.

'Hopefully, in the future, the Workshop will be at the frontier once again – but this time it will be a frontier shared with visuals, and once again we will be a sort of catalyst to encourage more experiments.'

# CHAPTER 6
## *The Concrete Mixers*

'If we can't call you composers,
then how about concrete mixers?'
*Geoffrey Manuel, Head of Programme Operations,*
*BBC Radio 1976*

As I've sat and watched various programmes on the Beeb, I've heard all sorts of synthesised burblings emanating from my humble TV set. When the credits roll, the mysterious name 'BBC Radiophonic Workshop' flashes by. I have to ask myself: 'Who are these strange people, employed in twiddling knobs for the aural delights of the British public?'

A. J. McIntyre of Wivenhoe asked the question in a letter to the Workshop in January 1982 – one of many that arrive in the Maida Vale postbag that echo a common query. No doubt about it: the unit holds a special fascination for many people who may know everything or nothing about electronic music but who respond to what they hear on BBC radio and television. Since the unit was first formed, many others have become professionally interested and have, in one way or the other, 'got into the act'. Polytechnics, universities, colleges and musical conservatories throughout the world now possess their own electronic equipment for music making. Some have elaborately equipped experimental studios; others run courses.

The world of pop music has taken to the new sounds in a very big way. Where the early enthusiasts of *musique concrète* and electronic sound may have had specialised taste, today it is the ordinary record-buyer who listens for pleasure to the sounds of individuals and groups working in the field of electronic-computer-synthesiser sound. Several albums of the Workshop's output are currently available, and one of them, *BBC Radiophonic Workshop – 21*, finds itself in the Top 100 list of a specialist supplier of electronic music.

Many letters come from fans of the long-running *Doctor Who* series, harking back to enquire just how Dick Mills contrived the sounds of The Krynoid lurching along the corridors of a country mansion where a mangling machine was busy in the basement!

Fourteen-year-old schoolboys who own their personal synthesisers and bedroom recording studios ask if they can come to visit the

Radiophonic Workshop and watch the composers at work. The answer to amateurs, most professionals and would-be Workshop employees alike has to be almost inevitably and invariably, a polite but firm 'No'.

Over twenty-five years many people have worked with radiophonic sound and music at Maida Vale and their talents, contributions and compositions have varied at different times and in different ways. Two factors unite them all: enthusiasm and practicality; the ability to create and the discipline to meet a deadline.

Desmond Briscoe says: There is always an element of experiment, and we have always been a pioneering place. But we rarely experiment just for its own sake. Every commitment is its own experiment. People often think that what we do is a team effort, but it isn't. A composer here at the Workshop has a very lonely job because from the moment that he has looked at the script or film and discussed it with the director, he is on his own.

The writer, confronted with a blank page, is not in half so daunting a situation as the composer because he has to create his orchestra before he starts. There are no reference books to help. If you are a designer working on a television play set in ancient Greece, then you can look up and find out exactly what buildings were like both from the outside and the inside; and the costume designer can also find out a great deal of what the people wore. The radiophonic composer may know all about ancient Greek Modes, but that is all the help he will get. This lack of instant reference has always been an additional problem – or at least something that has separated the Workshop from most other creative services within the media.

What *is* strange is that there is often a similarity in what people come up with when given the same task. We've had different composers asked to produce the sound of gold – and each one was recognisably similar. But that is radiophonic alchemy and not reference.

Another problem is time. It's no use sitting down for a week thinking artistic thoughts when you know that the programme deadline is just a week away. The philosophy of the Workshop has always been to provide a service, and as far as I am concerned, it must be an utterly reliable service. It doesn't matter how clever you are if the goods are not delivered on time – and they also have to be the right goods for that particular programme. If they don't work at first, then they have to be changed so that they are acceptable and workable within the production. In these days of multi-million-dollar co-productions there is an awful lot of responsibility hanging round your neck.

How then do people become radiophonic composers?

Desmond Briscoe: The people who work here all first come on attachment, maybe a week to start with. They have a look around and get the feel of the place, and we look at them to see if they will fit in. If there's promise, then they will be invited to come back for a longer attachment – usually for three months – during which time they will be expected to take a creative 'dogsbody' role.

As regards previous training, *some* are conventionally-trained musicians, but my experience over the years has convinced me that the trained musician can often be at a disadvantage. His mind has been set on certain lines and to obey certain rules. He is often unwilling to break them – or is unhappy if he does. The intuitive musician is sometimes the more imaginative.

Some of them are technically very clever, but all the Workshop asks for is a technical instinct. It really is not important for them to know in detail what happens inside the boxes. It is much more important for them to know which rules they can break and which they can't. They are, in many cases, jacks of all trades and – eventually – masters of making radiophonic music and special sound by art and by craft, and by doing everything themselves, successfully. Not just once, but time and time again. As Douglas Cleverdon once said in conversation here at the Workshop: 'Art is something that you do for the first time, and craft is the second, third and subsequent times'. The total staff of the Workshop – the permanent people, that is – has never exceeded twelve. Of those twelve, six are composers with studios of their own, and working alone; there are also two secretaries who look after everything and everybody; two engineers who assess, maintain, modify, develop and install equipment; the Organiser, responsible for the allocation of commitments, the provision of facilities and who deputises for the Head of Radiophonic Workshop whose responsibilities include the direction, development and professional standards of the department.

Originally we would take attachees – who mostly come from the ranks of radio studio managers, but by no means exclusively so – for six months. Some people were immediately unhappy when they found what they had let themselves in for, and disappeared after a few weeks. One chap left after only three days. So a staff decision was taken and it was agreed that people who wanted to learn the techniques and had what seemed to be the right approach and background would come initially for a week. During that week they would be given the space, time, and equipment to put something on tape if they wanted to. But more importantly, they would spend the week getting to know the permanent staff, and the staff could get to know them.

People have described the Workshop as being either a benevolent dictatorship or a workers' democracy. In the case of attachees we take a very democratic line and it is the staff that make the decision as to whether a person is invited back for a longer attachment. If they are not, then I am always prepared to tell them why. But if they do return, then it is usually for three months during which they work with everybody and for everybody. They do the copying, and some editing. They act as studio managers when people have musicians in to record. They also have the opportunity – with help and supervision – of doing their own shows, starting with easy ones and working to the more difficult commitments. They are also shown something of the way in which work is done for television, which is very important since many of the attachees come from radio.

The all-important element for Workshop composers is total self-motivation. They are all self-scheduling and have total freedom to work as and when they want to, by day or night, since the Workshop never closes. Though they do not necessarily always work on the programmes they themselves would choose, many commitments come about through previous good working relationships with particular producers. In radiophonic composition, as in the rest of life, there are definitely 'horses for courses'.

People generally tend to do what they do best as much as they can. But the final decision is with the Workshop's Organiser, Brian Hodgson, in consultation with Desmond Briscoe, a formidable but understanding partnership sometimes referred to as Desmond O'Brian, Merseyside entertainers and purveyors of radiophonic music to Royalty and the great British public!

Quite apart from self-motivation, the official job description of a composer at the Radiophonic Workshop is daunting. It consists of thirty separate categories of expertise which would deter many a strong and seemingly able man or woman from even bothering to apply. For example:

The producer/composer will be required to collaborate with writers, actors, graphic designers, film editors and of course radio and television producers. He will also be expected . . . to interpret programme requirements when the subjects are outside his own previous experience . . . to attend location shooting and be able to interpret visual images in sound terms from whatever source, eventually coming up with signature tunes, themes and incidental music for anything from a programme on the love life of a blood orange to an abstract ballet shot underwater. . . .

The composer will advise the programme producer on the booking of certain artists, musicians or actors; book special studio facilities; evolve, where necessary, an original system of notation or work with figures, frequencies or diagrams. . . . He will himself perform instrumentally or vocally or coach actors who are required to sing and who do not read music. . . . He will direct studio managers in music sessions, write parts for the musicians and direct them during recordings. . . . Quite frequently he will advise the programme producer on the use of radiophonic material during the recording in sound studio, dubbing theatre or television studio and also advise studio manager and dubbing mixer both technically and artistically. He may be required to 'conduct' studio musicians and 'cue-in' actors. . . .

Coping with considerable pressure is an important aspect of the work of a radiophonic composer, but he is also expected to pioneer new ideas and techniques, to develop and continue to acquire skills other than those expected in normal sound operational work and to investigate new commercial devices that could be suitable for the Workshop. . . .

He will also be expected, when required, to write and to broadcast on his work and to explain the Workshop to visitors and to various educational institutions and others who ask for lectures. . . .

Apart from the ability to cope with the foregoing, a producer/composer at the Radiophonic Workshop is expected to remain a fairly ordinary citizen who just happens to mow his lawn at hours which may seem odd to a 9-to-5 worker. A lady is, of course, entitled to maternity leave, but it is a great advantage if she just happens to have her own electronic equipment at home so that she does not become out of touch with the work she will be undertaking when she gets back to Maida Vale.

What the unit doesn't need are half a dozen Mozarts, though at least one Workshop composer says it would be interesting to have a Wagner or two since they would undoubtedly enjoy making powerful sounds on equipment that would leave the loudest and largest symphony orchestra sounding pitifully thin:

Desmond Briscoe: There's no doubt in my mind that if I recruited only people who could make great works of art, they would take a lot of time to make just one work and it would cost far too much. That sort of person would never be able to cope with fifty new pieces a year, each made with precise synchronisation for every type of programme from a cartoon film to experimental poetical drama. The people who work here provide a creative service with as much imagination and artistry as is possible within the constraints.

Apart from the creativity there's also the psychological wear and tear when deadlines loom and, because of the sheer

*Right:* Brian Hodgson in the 'sixties counting frames. One frame of film at 25 frames per second = .6 of an inch of magnetic tape at 15 inches per second. Counting frames individually was necessary before the Workshop became equipped with a film synchroniser

complexity of modern television production things are delayed. Then the time left for our contribution, which comes at the end of the process, can be very short indeed. The bigger the involvement of other people the more delays there are. Increasingly the physical methods of adding music and effects to programmes differ. In the past if the music was for a television documentary then you took your composition along on tape and it was played on a tape machine. For something more complex, on several tape machines. Nowadays producers may want the music as a guide track to filming before the production even comes into the studio.

They may also want different tracks for the studio work and different tracks again when it comes to the dub. So a Workshop composer is working not only to one deadline, but multiple deadlines. Fortunately, I think that's a stage which is already passing. Nowadays more producers are using synchronised systems of dubbing video and tape on multitrack, which means that very little music or sound is put on in advance. It's obviously a great help if a composer sitting in his studio in Maida Vale can work to the actual video with all the information on shape and timing before his eyes rather than just working from a script.

No matter how perfect the piece, and how pleased the radiophonic composer with his creation, it is never certain whether that's the way the composition will work in the programme. Programme producers have to be flexible and cut material if they think it necessary. The chances are that they will cut on a scene junction which is exactly where the music is, and so the radiophonic composer's timings may then be wrong. It is therefore very difficult for a Workshop composer to know if a particular job is actually completed, since the programme producer may well be making changes right up to the final dub.

I think that the first time a composer goes into a film cutting room must be a very distressing and traumatic experience. Here is their own beautiful music coming out of a moviola with a little tinny speaker and great clatterings of machine noise drowning half the details of their carefully constructed sounds. That is the first blow. Later, their music starts being cut about to fit the action!

On the whole there *must* be more satisfaction in actually doing the work than in the finished result as it is finally heard on radio and television, within the context of the programme. After all the radiophonic music and sound is only a small part of the whole and there must be compromise in programme making.

We try to balance this out by giving the composers at the Workshop the occasional opportunity to make their own extended pieces or programmes. They can be as lengthy and ambitious as they like providing that they can sell the idea to the BBC, in order that it may be broadcast when it is completed. Actually, we have been extremely successful in some of these projects.

### A Chorus of Glow-Worms

This was just one request amongst many on the Workshop's Log for April 1974. It came from Mary Haydon, a programme producer for Schools Radio, and the image had particular appeal, both then and now, for Desmond Briscoe. He was, admittedly, looking out for a collective name for his team at the time! They, on the other hand, were not necessarily convinced. Their argument ran: since we work alone, how can we be a chorus? And Glow-Worms?! What to call the people who actually make radiophonic music and sound has always been a problem, and at one time 'glow-worms' seemed just about as appropriate as anything since the battle had raged for years. Originally, everyone engaged in making sounds or music by radiophonic means was called an assistant, which was not really very descriptive of their activity, and became even more confusing when attachees were by definition assistants to assistants, and engineers were technical assistants assisting assistants to assistants.

(from left to right) Malcolm Clarke, Dick Mills and Brian Hodgson in 1969, at the Prevost, the Workshop's first film viewing machine

The Workshop's attempt to have people classified as 'composers' was finally thrown out by the BBC management. Composing, according to BBC definition, was something that you *do*, not something that you *are*. Not if you are a BBC person, anyway. Though the Corporation may commission outside 'composers' to compose music, there has never been a 'composer' as such on the permanent staff, though some BBC employees may well compose music whilst called something entirely different.

The then Director of Programmes Radio, Douglas Muggeridge, himself a great supporter of the Workshop and its aims, just couldn't stomach the idea of a BBC post called 'composer'. Eventually, after much exchange of ideas and musical philosophies, a compromise was reached. Since everyone agreed that people working on radiophonic music and sound were indeed 'composing', then they could be called, officially, 'Producers' (Radiophonic Music)! Honour was thus partially satisfied.

However, in the Workshop the 'producers' still tend to be referred to as composers, so there is no confusion between radiophonic composers/producers and programme producers. Nobody at the present time wants to start the argument again, even though a producer does tend to need company to do his producing, and a composer works alone.

> Desmond Briscoe: It has always been a very personal and very lonely job. The process happens largely in the head and is realised through the hands guided by the ears. Nobody else can do anything to help in that process. When the phones stop and the Workshop intercom is silent, and the building goes quiet, and the silence of night comes down, you can work in a much more concentrated way and often lose track of time completely.

In whatever silence they can achieve, and in the right frame of mind, the producers/composers of Maida Vale ponder over their three or four or five current commitments for radio and television programmes and prepare in their own individual ways, to make sounds out of the silence. The tunesmiths will work out their tunes. Others will concentrate on abstract sounds. The deep, dark, soul-searching sounds come easier these days on the synthesiser rather than by lengthy loops of tape. Whatever his personal method, and individual problems he has to solve, each composer works in his own studio with his own equipment. He has everything to hand except for the odd item of equipment, the special, one-off device, which is relatively portable and is moved from studio to studio as required.

> Desmond Briscoe: Each composer has his own way of working. There's the person who can sit at home, put down on manuscript paper what he wants, then come into the studio at nine o'clock in

the morning, put down the tracks, mix them together and go home at lunchtime. Then there's the person who comes in after lunch and appears to do nothing until tea-time when he has a gradual working-in process which reaches its creative peak at midnight and he goes home at four in the morning. There's the person who can turn out a short electronic pop signature tune in half a day and walk away from it leaving the radio and television programme producers with exactly what they wanted. There's the person who survives by the skin of his teeth all the time and combines instability with outstanding flair rather like a tightrope walker.

The person who gets cross and slams about and swears loudly and creates a lot of personal commotion doesn't tend to stay very long because he would exhaust himself if he did.

But every composer at the Workshop can come up against the period of tiredness. This is not always easy to detect since they work alone and are not likely to come around complaining. You notice the subtle difference when they start shouting about their equipment going wrong, and both of you know that there is nothing wrong with it at all; they are really shouting for help. That's when Brian Hodgson, Organiser, Radiophonic Workshop, and my deputy, and I can be of assistance. They can cry on either his shoulder or mine, depending on whom they blew off at first of all. Since we are involved on a day-to-day basis we can do this. A stranger would be just a nuisance. Like all families they squabble from time to time, but let anyone outside the family threaten us then everybody pulls together.

Apart from the day-to-day explosions of tiredness or temperament, there's also the question of how long a composer can stand, or wants to put up with, the pressures and pleasures of life at Maida Vale. Desmond Briscoe reckons that a career at the Workshop has peaks and troughs at fairly predictable times. Two years to gain real confidence. At three, the ability to tackle everything with ease and a broadening of range. From three to five years good solid work. From then on the possibility of encountering the psychological humps which you either get over or you don't. The really sophisticated work comes in between the seventh and the tenth year, and then they ask themselves the question: 'Do I really want to go on doing this till I'm sixty?' This is the critical period when people tend to move away to start their own studio, or to do their own thing in whatever way they choose.

# CHAPTER 7
## *Personages of Much Importance*

'. . . they are personages of much importance in the land,
although this may not be recognised. It matters little or nothing
to them whether it be recognised or not. In many ways I believe it is
desirable that they should continue in their comparative obscurity'.
*Lord Reith on 'broadcasters' in his book* Broadcast Over Britain

In his book, *Broadcast Over Britain*, Lord Reith, the first Director-General
of the BBC, wrote a paragraph about the broadcasters of his time that
could, by stretching a point or two, also be applied to the present-day
workers in radiophonic music and sound at Maida Vale.

For 'broadcasters', then, take your pick from all the descriptions
given to radiophonic composers – 'soundsmiths', 'tunesmiths',
'producers of radiophonic music', even 'concrete mixers'.

Lord Reith: The broadcasters are mostly young men. From the
nature of things in the beginning this was, I think, to be expected;
in view of the arduous and diverse nature of their labours it is
probably fortunate. They are rather shadowy personalities to the
average man; they are aloof and mysterious. You will probably
not find them at garden parties or social functions; their names
may not figure among the distinguished ones present, even if they
do go; most likely they are much too busy to spend their lives in
this way. (Yet) they are personages of much importance in the
land, although this may not be recognised. It matters little or
nothing to them whether it be recognised or not. In many ways I
believe it is desirable that they should continue in their
comparative obscurity.

Though Lord Reith referred only to young men, in radiophonic sound
and music young women have been equally important, both in the
early pioneering days and throughout the Workshop's twenty-five
years. He also used the word 'aloof', which would certainly not be true
of anyone working in the department today. Despite, or even perhaps
because of, the fact that they work so much alone, today's radiophonic
composers are only too happy to talk about the exigencies and
excitements of their work.

But certainly they do, like Lord Reith's broadcasters, remain
shadowy and mysterious – perhaps because of the Workshop's

reputation for science fiction, nightmare and nervous breakdowns! Not a lot is known publicly of who they are, how they came to the Workshop, how they go about their craft and art, and what they feel about it.

In this chapter, Desmond Briscoe introduces some of his colleagues, past and present. Firstly, Brian Hodgson, Liverpool-born and a showman by nature, who first came to Maida Vale in 1962 and having left the BBC in 1972 to start and run his own studio, returned in 1977, to be Organiser, Radiophonic Workshop, and deputy to Desmond Briscoe. Secondly Dick Mills, an irrepressible, imperturbable character, easy going and an expert on tropical fish, who is, next to Desmond, the Workshop's 'oldest inhabitant' and the man who has, since 1972, been especially involved with the special sounds for *Doctor Who*.

I suppose you could say that black magic helped Brian Hodgson towards a Workshop career, says Desmond Briscoe. When I first encountered him he had just completed a studio management course at the BBC's engineer training school at Evesham during which he had produced a most interesting programme on tape, that just happened to be about witchcraft and black magic. So I invited him to the Workshop for a chat. Then, shortly afterwards, I saw him acting in the BBC's own amateur company, the Ariel Players, whom he also directed in a musical show. Altogether it seemed to be an interesting combination of talents, so Brian eventually joined the Radiophonic Workshop, and afterwards John Baker, a sensitive man and a musician to his fingertips, who had written the show's music, was asked if he would like to come as well.

It was the start of a Workshop period with its own style and character. Despite the painstaking way that music and sound was made, everyone went about things in their own distinctive, artistic way. Dick Mills was our technical assistant, joining some six months after the Workshop first opened. Then a second operator came our way, John Harrison. John, who is tall and dark with a strong sense of propriety, was unusual in that he combined composing creativity with a technical ingenuity that proved absolutely essential at the time. Amongst his devices was a most useful one for switching variable speed tape machines so that they could be varied in semitones.

John also constructed mechanical devices for playing loops of tape and other contrivances that made it easier for us to achieve the sound that we wanted. But John was always deeply interested in the flora and fauna of the countryside, and it didn't come as a surprise when he elected to join the BBC's Natural History Unit in Bristol, where he is now a radio producer.

'Sound. What sound? That's the reaction I like to hear...'
*Brian Hodgson (1962–1972 and 1977 to date)*

I trained as an actor and earned my living at it until I joined the BBC. When I had to do my two years' National Service, I trained as an air wireless mechanic in the Royal Air Force. My electronic training was really very primitive and my musical training non-existent. But I did get a lot of opportunity to work with tape-recorders, which I found fascinating.

The area lying between sound and music became increasingly interesting to me, and that's the area into which I have channelled my creative output ever since. After joining the BBC and becoming a studio manager, Desmond invited me to the Workshop for a three-month attachment. Later, when he was looking for people with ideas, creative initiative and experience, it was agreed that I should stay longer – for quite a lot longer, as it was to turn out.

Then I left the BBC to run my own company for five years, working in the commercial field of electronic music.

Brian Hodgson

On first arriving at the Workshop, Brian found himself pitched straight in at the deep end with a brief to produce space-ship noises for a children's programme in the *Music and Movement* series. Though the Workshop has no official mottoes, one of them might well be: 'Deliver the goods and be positive about what you have done'.

When I had made the sounds I thought were right I played them to Vera Gray, the programme producer, and added: 'Well, of course, nowadays the eight-to-elevens actually understand a lot more about space than we do.' There was a pause, during which Vera Gray considered how best she could phrase her reply, and then she said: 'Yes, I'm sure they do – but this programme happens to be for the four-to-nine year olds.' Actually the space-ship sounds worked well anyway and the children liked them.

After that it was more drama for radio, and then for television, until another lady producer came into my life. Her name was Verity Lambert and she had a children's series that was to last for a few weeks and it was to be called *Doctor Who*. For the next nine years, this series took up a quarter of my time. When I wasn't doing *Doctor Who* then I was working with programme producers such as Philip Saville and Patrick Garland on quite different commitments, since I was always interested in the use of sound to create other dimensions.

Sometimes, the day after transmission of a production on which I had been working hard for a long time, someone would mention: 'That was an amazing play last night,' and I would reply: 'Yes, it was – and what did you think of the sound?' They would often reply: 'Sound? What sound?' At that point I knew that it had worked, because they were not aware of my contribution, but only of the programme as a whole. That's the joy for me – to have been a successful part of something that had finally come together, the total value transcending the sum of all the parts.

It has always continued to amaze me that the Workshop has existed for twenty-five years with all sorts of different people coming and going or staying on and working with different equipment, and it still provides something that satisfies the producer who has come to us and asked: 'Can you make me something that is right for this play?' The programme producer actually goes away with something that we have made for him that is magical and wondrous and exciting and expands the dimensions of the drama – and we still don't know how we have done it.

In radio and television there are many different brains working on the same thing. This is quite different from someone writing a book, or a composer working out his music. Together, a number of people are creating an experience for the listener and viewer and using a lot of complex equipment to do it.

This is why I have such a big bee in my bonnet about equipment and have made myself become interested in it, and tried to understand it, because the better the equipment we have, the less we filter ideas and emotions and the more directly we can convey them.

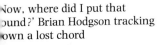

Now, where did I put that sound?' Brian Hodgson tracking down a lost chord

It was certainly a direct experience when I heard radiophonic sound for the first time: I was absolutely shattered! I was brought up during the war in Liverpool and the whole family's entertainment revolved around the radio. It was there for the news, of course, but also for amusement. There was *Music Hall*, and *Saturday Night Theatre*, and serious music and dance bands.

Then I remember listening to a programme called *Private Dreams and Public Nightmares* and being completely amazed by it. That was when I first heard radiophonic sound, and when I joined the BBC and eventually received Desmond's invitation to join his Workshop, I didn't hesitate.

In those early days, listeners who reacted as Brian Hodgson did to *Private Dreams and Public Nightmares* were in the minority. Many just couldn't fit pictures to the sounds and were driven to writing abusive letters complaining about 'mad and nightmarish' noises. But the pioneers were fortunate in that the BBC and its programme producers were at that particular time interested in the experimental, and they rode out the criticism rather grandly in the chariots of the avant-garde.

Brian Hodgson (left) working on the Dybbuk in Studio E with freelance music director Steven Deutsch

Nowadays, a whole generation has been weaned on radiophonic music and electronic sound. Children throughout the United Kingdom have grown up with *Listen with Mother* and other programmes where electronic sounds were an aid to learning and understanding as well as magic carpets to faraway places and the inner worlds of their own imaginations. Giants and spacemen moved with appropriate radiophonic noises, *Blue Peter's* Bleep and Booster were friendly and their electronic sounds welcome to the ear. Most of all, *Doctor Who* arrived in the living-room regularly each week with a signature tune which took them comfortably through time and space. What may be surprising to most people is that the Workshop spends about a quarter of its time dealing with educational programmes. The ability to amaze is now harnessed to the ability to instruct.

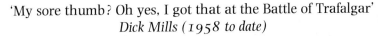

'My sore thumb? Oh yes, I got that at the Battle of Trafalgar'
*Dick Mills (1958 to date)*

Dick Mills

The first time that Dick Mills came into contact with the output of the Radiophonic Workshop was when he was working at Broadcasting House as a recording engineer, and had to fill in for someone who was off sick. The radiophonic tapes he had to play were for a science fiction story of two men who went by rocket to the moon and fell in love with a moon maiden. Both men came back pregnant!

This seemed to be expanding the imagination and the horizons of broadcasting, Dick thought. Shortly afterwards when a vacancy arose for someone to give technical assistance at the Workshop he decided to take a chance on it.

Dick had served with the Royal Air Force during his national service, and had been trained as a ground wireless mechanic. So when he came out he decided against a return to his former job in an insurance office in the City. 'I'd got rather fed up with being allowed to wear a sports jacket only on Saturday mornings. The rest of the week you mustn't ever take your suit jacket off in case a passing member of the public saw a City insurance worker improperly dressed.'

Dick joined the Workshop in 1958 about six months after it started and at that time each commission was undertaken by two people – the studio manager who did the creative work, and who was responsible for thinking up ideas for the sound sequence, and the technical assistant, who looked after the 'plugging' of the machines and also tackled some editing and sound treatments. As technical assistant Dick made sure that everything in the Workshop was lined up and ready to go every morning, tying up the loose ends left around after the 'masterpieces' of the night before had been created.

We work unusual hours, and all of us are different in our approach to our work, our attitudes and styles. If you could bottle up creativity and turn it on from nine a.m. until five in the evening when you switch off, that would certainly be appreciated by our long-suffering wives and families. But the television service imposes its own demands and timings. So often we are working at Maida Vale from Monday to Friday and then at BBC Television Centre on Saturday and Sunday. Since you can't be cut off in your creative prime just because it is half past five, most composers here will ride their creative wave until it peters out. *Then* they go home.

One important thing to remember is that everyone who works here is here for two reasons: they wanted to come, and Desmond Briscoe chose them to stay. Whether they were just always the right people for the job, people who could make the right decisions and had the right talents, or whether they evolved into that sort of person I just don't know. Is it nature, or nurture? Job influence or job training?

In 1982 the Technical Workshop was converted into Studio D which is mainly used by Dick Mills who is seen here (right) with Brian Hodgson inspecting the new mixing desk

In every programme we work on, each composer has an important responsibility, and it is up to him to contribute in a way that no one else can. Each composer tackles his commitments in his own way. So feeling unwell doesn't alter the fact that you have to deliver to the deadline and no one else can do it for you because no one else knows along which lines you were working.

One incident that brought home to me just how involved one gets in one's work happened when we did the Thomas Hardy story about the Battle of Trafalgar which went out on radio as *England's Harrowing*.

We had to create the sound of the main-mast collapsing at the Battle of Trafalgar. It was shot away by a cannon-ball and crashed down with the twenty-three sailors who were standing on the yardarm at the time. We did this sound by demolishing a long piece of four-by-four timber: physically rending it apart. The splinters, like the sound, were for real and I gashed myself on the thumb which was painful at the time but I soon forgot all about it. A week or so later my wife and I were standing in our local post office in one of the many queues that seemed to be going nowhere, and my wife asked: 'Where did you get that nasty gash in your thumb?', and I replied, without thinking: 'Oh, I did that at the Battle of Trafalgar.' Suddenly the queue evaporated around us and we were at the counter before I realised why!

## The man who sank the *Titanic*
### *Norman Bain*

Norman Bain

When Desmond Briscoe was appointed to run the Workshop he soon surrounded himself with talented people. Some were already working with the unit. Others were fellow experimenters from pre-Workshop days who came on attachment for a while and then went on their way. More arrived according to that strange natural law that draws creative people together when the time is right.

Norman Bain had been a colleague of Desmond's in Broadcasting House, a studio manager and one of the handful of broadcasters involved in the pioneering programmes *All That Fall*, *Private Dreams and Public Nightmares* and the radio plays of Giles Cooper. Over the years Norman had learned in a hard school the craft and art of manipulating sounds: he was very adept at it. He had also formed close working relationships with some of the foremost poets and playwrights then active in radio. Louis MacNeice was one such man. Though his plays did not require the same radiophonic treatment as Giles Cooper's, MacNeice's poetical radio dramas were enormously influential and successful.

Norman Bain: It was MacNeice who first put into a play a very little-known fact about the sinking of the *Titanic*. He decided for the purposes of his play that the iceberg didn't just get in the *Titanic*'s way, but was steered on a direct collision path by radio control. I was in charge of the sound of the engine room!

No similar disasters occurred during Norman Bain's time at Maida Vale. 'He was always,' says Desmond Briscoe, 'of very considerable help at a very important time in the Workshop's history.'

Norman himself, now a studio manager with the Quality Check Unit at Broadcasting House, remembers the early days of the newly formed Workshop with particular affection. 'I suppose that I met more creative people doing experimental work then, than I have in subsequent years.'

### Alias Ray Cathode
#### *Maddalena Fagandini (1960–1963)*

Making radiophonic music and sound has never been a purely masculine preserve. Daphne Oram was one of the pioneers of the field. Later, in 1960, Maddalena Fagandini joined the department and remained for three years, producing some very memorable pieces.

'She was – and still is,' says Desmond Briscoe, 'a lady of considerable talent and spirit.'

It was Maddalena who first brought the Workshop into the world of pop music with a catchy little interval signal later to be called *Time Beat*. It wasn't the first interval signal produced at the Workshop, nor was it Maddalena's first since at that time the BBC Television Service needed many such little pieces of catchy sound to fill the gaps between programmes.

Maddalena Fagandini

When a music publisher caught on to the possibility of Maddalena's piece, and the BBC agreed to a record, it was produced by George Martin (later to produce the Beatles) on the Parlophone label, credited to Ray Cathode. *Time Beat* was played by many of the disc jockeys of the day, was featured by David Jacobs on *Juke Box Jury*, and generally created a considerable amount of interest in what the Workshop was doing. It was a landmark of its kind, even though it didn't get a very high placing in the charts.

Amongst the productions that Maddalena remembers with most pleasure was *Rhinoceros*:

It took us two whole weeks to find the right sounds for their hooves, then we had to transform actors' voices ('rhinocerify' them) and make a troop of the beasts waltz and march and crash into things.

A series called *Things That Go Bump In The Night* – real ghost stories from the BBC Archives – affected us so much when we were providing music and sound to go with it, that the eerie sounds we

*Time Beat* the Workshop's first pop record, and Ray Cathode's only claim to fame

made were in direct line with how scared we felt, working late at night in Maida Vale.

Maddalena composed music for *Insect Play* in 1960, and did some of her most rewarding work for the radio adaptation of Jean Cocteau's famous film *Orphée*. Using plucked piano strings she worked for three weeks with an obscure ancient Greek enharmonic scale to produce the chilling and passionate theme for the Princess of Death.

> Desmond Briscoe: Maddalena was always being stolen from us because she was bilingual. We lost her to Outside Broadcasts for the Olympic Games in Rome and then to television to work on the Italian language series *Parliamo Italiano*. Finally we lost her completely and she eventually became a television producer of Continuing Education programmes.

### Jenyth Worsley (1961–1962)

Another young lady to make her mark with the Workshop at this time was Jenyth Worsley, who having composed the memorable *Magic Carpet* for Schools Radio department's *Music and Movement*, left the unit to become a producer in that department and eventually to 'drag *Listen with Mother* screaming from the womb into the 1970s'. She remained its producer, and as such a Workshop customer for many years.

### The man who said 'No' to a Knee-Cap Sonata!
### John Baker (1963–1974)

> You *do* meet a lot of nut-cases in electronic music. I suppose you're bound to when people are exploring their own fields, but I promise you that one man from the Royal Shakespeare Company wanted me to make him a piece of music from the noise of his knee-caps moving.

Jenyth Worsley

Though Baker used all manner of things to make his sounds, on that occasion he demurred. '*You* record your knee-cap, and I'll do my best,' he replied – and never heard from the chap again.

Though he never produced the Knee-Cap Sonata, John Baker's tuneful and witty pieces often had as their starting point a natural sound which he then scored in the traditional way on normal music manuscript paper. His famous call sign for Radio Nottingham used the sound of blowing across the neck of a bottle; *Sea Sports* and *Reading Your Letters* started with the sound of a cork being pulled from a bottle. *New Worlds* was based on the sound of a metal spring being released.

John studied at the Royal Academy of Music, and joined the BBC in 1960. He came to the Workshop in 1963 and immediately began to specialise in signature tunes for radio and television programmes, writing more or less conventional music but with unusual sound qualities.

John Baker

Desmond Briscoe: John is a superb pianist and very interested in jazz. He could do anything on a keyboard, but he found his first year at the Workshop difficult because he couldn't find a swift way from the Royal Academy training and jazz techniques to electronic music. John Harrison who was here at the same time, helped out a lot, and John Baker eventually worked out systems which are still known as 'Baker techniques' to people here today.

He would go through his score recording all the different pitches of the notes he wanted. He would write for three tape-recorders playing together and sit there and edit whilst listening to something else. He even got to the point where it seemed he didn't need to measure the notes to produce syncopation, but could just do it by eye!

*Inset:* John Baker in 1965 re-routing a sound

*Below:* John Baker in 1974 working at the 'Glowpot Desk', the Workshop's light-operated mixer

John developed this to a fine art and produced an enormous amount of very tuneful music that was just right for the time. It was John Baker who composed and realised the first signature tune for the original *PM* programme which ran for many years.

### 'Our only living medieval composer'
### *David Cain (1967–1973)*

David Cain was our only living medieval composer. He looked the part, being heavily bearded and inclined to fits of wild emotion but with a tremendous charm. He was the first person to make us realise the importance of each composer having a studio of his own. He would growl at people to keep them out.

Desmond Briscoe continues: I first met David at a concert of electronic music at Newbury in Berkshire. Organised by Peter Zinovieff, Delia Derbyshire and Brian Hodgson, it was a good concert and I remember that Sir John Betjeman was there and I often wondered what he thought of it.

David, a mathematician from Imperial College, was a self-taught jazz and big-band musician, playing double-bass and guitar. At one time he was purely into jazz, but then he met the late David Munrow, who introduced him to early music. Cain was immediately hooked, and became fascinated by the sound of medieval instruments.

Like many other Workshop people, he was a BBC studio manager before moving to Maida Vale. His first big project after he arrived in 1967 was the eight-part radio serial *The War of the Worlds*, for which he composed mainly electronic music. Then he tackled Tolkien's *The Hobbit*, in which he changed his style and attempted 'a reality which nobody could pinpoint as having anything to do with our world'. The music was a mixture of medieval instruments and electronics and made a big impact when it was broadcast, though undoubtedly he will be best remembered for his radio adaptation, composition and production of the Asimov *Foundation Trilogy*.

For the BBC Radio Schools series *Drama Workshop* David contributed excitingly imaginative radiophonic music – again with a medieval flavour. It was released on a BBC Records LP entitled *The Seasons*, produced by David Lyttle and with poems by Ronald Duncan.

David Cain became the second member of the Workshop to leave (in 1973) and receive a Gulbenkian Grant (the first was Daphne Oram). He now teaches with the Cumbrian Education Authority and still writes incidental music for radio, 'some of it instrumental and conventional and some, highly unconventional'.

### At the sign of the green lampshade
#### *Delia Derbyshire (1962–1973)*

It's a suitable name for legends; and certainly a number of anecdotes about Delia crop up in any reminiscences of the time when she – together with Desmond Briscoe, Brian Hodgson, John Baker and David Cain – formed what some people look back upon as one of the golden ages of the Radiophonic Workshop.

One tale concerns her creation of the biggest loop of recording tape ever seen in the history of the world. It circled her studio several times, looped gracefully out of the door and down the corridor as far as the commissionaire's desk at the entrance of BBC Maida Vale Studios, and back again. Not everyone totally believes that one.

Another story concerns her minor classic of radiophonic music, the signature tune to *Great Zoos of the World.* It was apparently created overnight, with a little help from her friends, and completed just in time for the surprised and delighted programme producer who had come up specially from Bristol to take away a piece created entirely from the sounds of real animals.

Delia Derbyshire

Born in Coventry, and trained as a pianist, Delia read mathematics and music at Cambridge University and joined the Workshop team in 1962. Delia came to us very highly qualified indeed, says Desmond Briscoe. At first she asked whether she could spend her

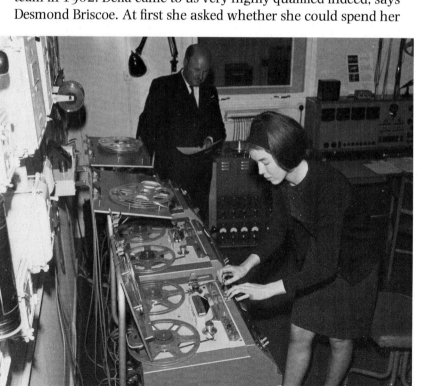

Delia Derbyshire in 1965 editing on the Philips tape-recorders. These were the first 'hi-fi' tape-recorders to arrive at the Radiophonic Workshop. Behind her is Desmond Briscoe who is standing by the first eight-track recorder to be purchased by the BBC

days off sitting quietly in a corner and watching us work. We replied: 'Yes of course.' So this tall, quiet, auburn-haired young lady came over from Broadcasting House whenever she wasn't working as a studio manager, and watched us. Later she stayed on to contribute an enormous amount of very beautiful – almost unearthly – and quite remarkable music. Some of her pieces like *The Delian Mode* and *Blue Veils and Golden Sands* are without parallel in our output.

Few people can write witty music, but Delia could. She was an original worker who used an analytical approach to synthesise complex sounds from electronic sources. The mathematics of sound came naturally to her and she could take a set of figures and build them into music in a way quite different from anyone else.

Delia was also one of the first people to overcome the criticism that radiophonic music was always horrific. She really gave the lie to that often repeated saying that it was easy to be horrid, reasonably easy to be amusing, pretty difficult to be pompous and grandiose, and very difficult indeed to be beautiful.

It was Delia who first realised electronically Ron Grainer's music for the *Doctor Who* signature tune. Delia's ability to take on enormous projects to order was to be shown again much later when she composed a special extended electronic piece for the Institute of Electrical Engineers which was performed before the Queen and Prince Philip at the Royal Festival Hall. Taking the initial letters IEE, Delia composed music from their mathematical correspondences and from morse code; introducing elements of the development of electricity in communication from the earliest telephone to the Americans landing on the moon. There was the voice of Mr Gladstone congratulating Mr Edison on inventing the phonograph; the opening and closing down of Savoy Hill with Lord Reith's voice: and Neil Armstrong speaking as he stepped onto the surface of the moon. The powerful punch of Delia's rocket take-off threatened the very fabric of the Festival Hall.

Her collaboration with writer Barry Bermange on the Third Programme series of four programmes called *Inventions for Radio*, was most distinguished. For *Dreams*, Bermange had first recorded a number of people talking about their dreams and then analysed the resulting conversations into subjects. Together, he and Delia built up a word pattern which was then set to pure electronic sound. For the second programme in the series *Amor Dei* it was decided to use no electronic sounds at all. At one point, Barry Bermange said that he would like 'the sound of a Gothic altarpiece'. 'Show me,' said Delia. So Bermange drew a beautiful Gothic altarpiece and said: '*That* sort of sound.' Using human voices

2

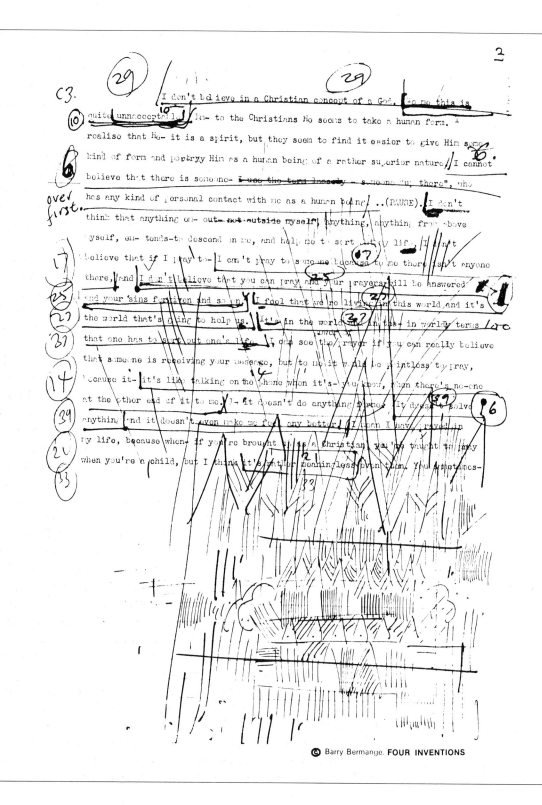

C3.

I don't believe in a Christian concept of a God. To me this is quite unacceptable. In- to the Christians He seems to take a human form. I realise that He- it is a spirit, but they seem to find it easier to give Him some kind of form and portray Him as a human being of a rather superior nature. I cannot believe that there is someone- I use the term loosely - someone "up there", who has any kind of personal contact with me as a human being ..(PAUSE). I don't think that anything on- out- not outside myself, anything, anything from above myself, en- tends-to descend on me, and help me to sort out my life. I don't believe that if I pray to- I can't pray to someone because to me there isn't anyone there, and I don't believe that you can pray and your prayers will be answered and your sins forgiven and so on. I feel that we are living in this world and it's the world that's going to help us. It's in the world and in the- in worldly terms that one has to sort out one's life. I can see the prayer if you can really believe that someone is receiving your message, but to me it would be pointless to pray, because it- it's like talking on the phone when it's- you know, when there's no-one at the other end of it to me. I- it doesn't do anything either. It doesn't solve anything, and it doesn't even make me feel any better. I mean I have prayed in my life, because when- if you're brought up as a Christian you're taught to pray when you're a child, but I think it's rather meaningless even then. You sometimes-

© Barry Bermange. **FOUR INVENTIONS**

and developing the use of sung words on tape, Delia provided what he wanted.

That was music to take seriously, of course, says Delia. But I always immensely enjoyed doing funny programmes. There was one called *Family Car*, a do-it-yourself maintenance programme, for which they wanted lighthearted cartoon-type music. I worked out the four-stroke cycle of an engine and made suitable push . . . suck . . . bang . . . blow . . . noises. I used the tune *Get Out and Get Under*, but I made it on simulated car horns and cut it together very carefully. The music worked all right, but it was turned down because one particular car had been used for the series and the manufacturers didn't really want my efforts to be associated with their product.

A classic case of 'coals to Newcastle' occurred during this time following a visit to the Workshop by a freelance German broadcaster. His interviews with the Maida Vale radiophonic music composers were built into a radio programme which proved so successful that Munich Radio approached the BBC with a polite request for a radiophonic signature tune for their daily news programme, which had since the war been heralded by an Eric Coates March. The BBC agreed, and the Workshop accepted the commission eagerly, thinking it an honour to be asked to export electronic sounds to the country that had first pioneered them. Delia Derbyshire composed the theme, and on the first evening that it was heard on air the German announcer duly credited and thanked the 'Britisher' lady composer who was responsible for the piece. Delia was also involved in yet another export to Germany when material composed at the Workshop was heard at the Festival of Electronic Music in Berlin. She reported back, the BBC's Radiophonic sounds were one thing: electronic 'art' music quite another.

There is always a certain satisfaction in attempting the near-impossible. Amongst the programmes I most enjoyed doing at Maida Vale was one for television about the Tuareg tribe. This contained some stunningly beautiful images and very long shots: like the thin line of a camel train crossing the desert in the heat of the sun. This to me was a very thin high sound. So I measured out the pace of the camels' feet on the film and made my music to fit them exactly. The rhythm that you hear is not me singing the tune. I recorded just one note and cut it up and speed-changed it, and then cut it into an obbligato rhythm. The electronic part was a very thin sound made by using all the filters in the Workshop and passing the sound through them in sequence.

That is one of the main reasons that I always seemed to end up working at night. I used so much equipment that I had to wait until everyone else had gone so that I could borrow it.

*Left*: Barry Bermange's Gothic altarpiece

At the end of the Tuareg sequence there is a most beautiful shot of one man with his blue cloak billowing out, and my thought was to find a beautiful sound and then make it swirl. My most beautiful sound at that time was made by a tatty green BBC lampshade which was lying around the studio. It was the wrong colour, but it had the most beautiful ringing sound to it. I hit the lampshade, recorded that, and then faded up the sound into the ringing part without the percussive start. I analysed the sound into all its partials and all its frequencies. Then I took the twelve strongest partials and reconstructed this sound on the Workshop's famous twelve oscillators to give a 'whooshing' sound.

So the camels rode off into the sunset with my voice in their hooves and green lampshades on their backs!

An Eastern note was also needed for *The Cyprian Queen*, a radio play produced by Michael Bakewell. I felt that this needed the quality of a flute, but disembodied and with a slightly Eastern note. The Workshop was like spaghetti junction as a result, with my loops of tape everywhere until I had finished.

Knowing when to stop is very important. When, for instance, I worked on a television film called *The Trans-Arctic Polar Walk* by Wally Herbert, I was able to find my sound and find my mode, and I recorded all night towards what I wanted; but when the dawn came I felt I had so much more that I needed to do. Then the cleaning lady came in and I asked her what the music reminded her of. 'The North Pole,' she replied. Right, I thought, I'm not going to muck about with it any longer.

Where other Workshop composers think in terms of visual images or colours, Delia considered everything in a very analytical way. 'Perhaps,' she said, 'I have a very strange mind because I analyse everything, not just music. The pace, the cutting, the editing of a film – even when I'm listening to the news I note every inflexion, every comma. There are so many subtleties in the human voice. I suppose in a way I was experimenting in psycho-acoustics.'

Delia left the Workshop in 1973.

Composition for crunched celery
*Richard Yeoman-Clark (1970–1978)*

When Richard – ex-chorister and backroom boy – first came to the Workshop on a week's attachment, Desmond Briscoe remembers, he spent four days of that week making a device in the technical workshop to make a piece of music within the week.

That seemed the right sort of balance we needed at the time, since I certainly needed to update our technical support; someone who could understand the relationship between technicalities and

Richard Yeoman-Clark

techniques. BBC Engineering gave a special sort of dispensation that he should be allowed to involve himself with engineering matters as well as programmes, and eventually he became an assistant and then a producer.

Richard was enormously able, with a dry sense of humour, and was very much involved in the theatre. He was responsible for the lighting and sound installations at the Abbey Theatre, St Albans: the theatre and the Workshop seemed to be his whole life.

Yeoman-Clark helped move the Workshop into the transistor age. As well as producing his own musical pieces he was of particular assistance during the remaking of three radio classics – *The Disagreeable Oyster*, *All That Fall* and *Under the Loofah Tree*; and also helped on the stereo version of Desmond Briscoe's *Narrow Boats* programme about the inland waterways of England. He balanced out these more traditional examples of the Workshop's output by working on one of the most avant-garde pieces attempted at Maida Vale – Lily Greenham's *Relativity*, an 'exploration' realised at the Workshop where the basic elements were spoken words and parts of words . . . to be listened to rather as music than a poetic work.

When Brian Hodgson became the Workshop's Organiser, Richard was able to relax his previous function as 'the Workshop's technical look-out or facilities man acting as a link between the creative staff, the engineering staff and the outside world of electronic and sound studios', and concentrate fully on creative contributions.

Richard Yeoman-Clark programming the Delaware with reduction mixer and keyboard in the foreground

Having arrived at the Workshop at about the same time as synthesisers he used the new equipment to good effect on such programmes as the space series *Blake's Seven*, and – in sharp contrast – did a setting of an Edward Lear poem for *The Space Between*. But he was not so obsessed with the new freedoms afforded by the synthesisers that he neglected the older, traditional techniques of *musique concrète*. He has even been known to create a composition from the noises made by crunching a stick of celery.

Richard left the workshop in 1978 to take charge of the technical maintenance at a major London Recording Studio.

### 'Raping the muse . . .'
### *Paddy Kingsland ( 1970–1981 )*

'The reason that I took up electronic music,' Paddy Kingsland wrote in answer to an enthusiast's letter to him at the Workshop, 'was that it seemed a good idea at the time.'

Paddy was previously a BBC tape editor and then a studio manager, chiefly with Radio 1. His interest in radio had started very early. When he was about thirteen he had not only learned the basics of electricity and radio and the skills needed to make amplifiers and bits and pieces with a soldering iron, but he was also a pop group guitarist just before the era of the Beatles.

During the eleven years he worked at the Maida Vale unit he contributed largely to the Radiophonic Workshop's life and lore, creating many hours of music for all types of programmes. Before leaving in 1981 in order to set up his own commercial studio producing electronic music, he had gained a considerable reputation for his work on *The Hitch-Hiker's Guide to the Galaxy* and also produced an ambitious rock musical for radio *Rockoco*.

Paddy Kingsland at his desk in Studio E in 1980

> Desmond Briscoe: Paddy came to us with a big reputation in the pop world as a performer and disc jockey in his own right. He had his own disc jockey set-up and used to tour around in a huge van. He was a professional guitarist, and took up playing the synthesiser almost as soon as it was invented.
>
> He definitely had a style of his own, and was one of the first people to use percussion, bass, horns and trumpets – all sorts of instrumental sounds – mixed in with his electronic music. Certainly he was able to make a very commercial product.
>
> Says Paddy: I'm very fortunate in that I actually do enjoy the sort of things that I do, and don't in any way consider jobs to be just bread-and-butter work until I can produce that great long masterpiece. I rarely write anything that is not specifically to order. That's why the Workshop suited me so well: it was – and still is – providing music very particularly for other people, and to

be used in a certain definite way. Which is quite different from the great classical composers who, though they might have been asked for music for a purpose or for a patron, were still writing primarily for themselves.

Workshop music must create moods and atmospheres, it must be of a specific length and fit exactly with predetermined pictures or dialogue. It is very important not to dismiss such good workmanlike jobs as pieces of music, just because they have no pretensions. The Workshop has always been interested in technique and timing, the relationships between spoken word and music, pictures and music, the balance between the various instruments and the way that things are put together.

Nowadays you can achieve much more than ever before in adding texture to sound. You can give all sorts of treatment to an instrument. In a simple case, you can add echo to a flute. Then leave something else – like a voice or maybe a guitar – absolutely dry, with no echo on it at all. This would not have been possible years ago, and it has created textures which are of interest in their own right.

I've always been amazed at the number of people who will take the trouble to write in to the BBC saying how much they've enjoyed something and where could they get the record. Sure, we occasionally got complaints – and took them very seriously. This response from the listeners and viewers was an attractive aspect of working for the Radiophonic Workshop; but I suppose that the order and discipline of working to a deadline was the biggest spur.

A remark I heard from a musical arranger summed it up well. He said that most people working professionally in the field of music couldn't just wait for the Muse to come along to them. It was more a question of frantically raping the Muse at the last minute to get the result you want.

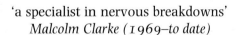

'a specialist in nervous breakdowns'
*Malcolm Clarke (1969–to date)*

At one time in his Workshop career, Malcolm Clarke appeared to have cornered the market in deteriorating states of mind. He had just worked on three plays in a row which involved characters cracking up. When people asked him what he did for a living, he would reply that he specialised in nervous breakdowns.

Afterwards Malcolm reflected: Perhaps it was something to do with my education. For 'A' levels I did Physics, Art and Music – a combination which many schools would have considered to be a sign of schizophrenia. It certainly broadened my mind but wasn't much help when it came to getting a job. The real reason I came to

Malcolm Clarke

89

the BBC was that I didn't really know what I wanted to do and thought that if I couldn't find a satisfying job within such a huge organisation then it was I who was at fault.

Fortunately, Clarke combines a number of talents and enthusiasms which proved useful. Interested in putting sounds together from a very early age, he joined the engineering department of the BBC, then became a studio manager and came to the Workshop in 1969.

Apart from David Cain, who set himself up in a studio and metaphorically barred the door against all comers, Malcolm was the person who most wanted to establish a place of his own where he could 'hang up his hat', says Desmond Briscoe.

He has always been a highly imaginative, temperamental and original worker who possesses the mind's ear of both a serious composer and a child. This makes it possible for him to produce music which is both witty and fantastic and often exquisitely beautiful.

His interest in art makes Malcolm Clarke the right composer to support the visual element in programmes about art, and several radio documentaries have contained outstanding examples of his work: including programmes on the artists Constable, Picasso, Klee and Dali.

But it was neither harrowing mind-drama, nor fine art programmes or children's programmes (another Clarke speciality) that brought him into the public eye. Once again it was that long-time Workshop favourite genre, the science fiction story. Not just *any* old story, but the Ray Bradbury classic *There Will Come Soft Rains*. The story had already come to the Workshop for radiophonic treatment on two previoius occasions. This time Malcolm adapted it under the title *August 2026*, and it won him an award from the Society of Authors.

When I first joined the Workshop, says Malcolm, I remember being shown oscillators and white noise generators and things to enable them to be switched on or off in an acceptable fashion. That, I was told, was the Workshop. Not so! I thought. As a listener I have been hearing all sorts of exciting sounds which didn't seem to be just electronic – there must be more to it than that equipment.

We had a saying in those days that we were working at the frontiers and we ought to be able to claim travelling expenses 'to the frontier and back'. There was certainly a pioneering spirit and a great delight in doing things for the first time with the equipment at our disposal. But there were boundaries imposed by that equipment and you could solve a problem up to a certain point but after that you knew that you couldn't improve on it. Nowadays I do not know the immediate answers since there are so many possibilities.

What is happening in the technical world is both exciting and frightening because technology is developing step by step in a scientific way, and not in an artistic way. As soon as one problem has been posed in technical terms, it is almost as quickly solved. Technical progress is shooting ahead in a straight line whereas art doesn't work like that; it works in a nebulous, airy-fairy way. We don't, as artists, think in straight lines but laterally, and backwards and forwards – all over the place in fact. With the pace of modern technology there is a very real danger that we can't feel

*Left:* Malcolm Clarke loading the autolocator in Studio C – a device for locating a specific place on the tape

*Below:* Malcolm Clarke editing a sound on The Prophet V synthesiser

the framework within which we are working any more because it is for ever moving away from us.

I think my early training in fine art encouraged me to be only satisfied with an end product that I could hold up to my public and say: 'This is a piece of me, like it or leave it.' The Radiophonic Workshop is the only area in radio that I have discovered where one can make such a complete art form, starting from the raw materials and at the end of the day having the finished product with no one else having been involved.

Everything I hear I translate into visual terms and I can discuss sound problems in visual terms very happily indeed. That's a big purple square sound, or whatever.

In the composition of electronic music there is nothing to be done until one has a sound to refer to. So I start off with a sound which will be useful to me, a sound which generates the right mood. Here again the rules of art apply: short wave high frequency sounds tend to be blue and cold. Low frequency sounds tend towards red and warmth and – dare we say it – sex! In a disco you can have blue lights and red lights flashing, but the red lights are more exciting. Bass frequencies are very fundamental and physical – body rhythms and particularly low frequencies do very strange things to us. High frequencies can be quite painful, but we can reject them, and that makes them more acceptable. Lower frequencies become part of the body and when one starts duplicating the pulse rate and other low rhythmic ideas then we are into very interesting but potentially exciting areas.

'The trouble with the future is that you never know fully
about it until you've passed it . . .'
*Roger Limb (1972–to date)*

A prolific composer, says Briscoe, Roger is a professionally trained musician who has always played or taught or been involved with music as a living or for pleasure. He learned to play the piano at four or five years of age, was improvising and composing pop numbers at thirteen, and playing double bass with great success in the Grammar School Orchestra at about the same time. In the evenings he was playing jazz, which together with pop music was an important influence in his formative years.

Roger Limb studied music at university; moved to London to work as a music teacher in Islington and all the time was playing jazz gigs up and down the country and abroad. 'By this time I was getting dog tired of all the travelling so I joined the BBC as a studio manager in Belfast. Not that it was as easy as that; the BBC had turned me down at first and

Roger Limb

I had reconciled myself to continuing to teach.'

In Belfast Roger gained experience of television, working as vision-mixer on the evening magazine programme. Later he moved to Birmingham 'to fade up Dan Archer's cows' for eighteen months, before coming to London again, this time to Bush House where he stayed for five years with the BBC Overseas Service. He gained practical experience in studio techniques, and at the same time had a London base from which to play spare-time gigs. 'I was sort of first reserve bass player for the Chris Barber Jazz Band for many years and I did quite a bit of backing for pop – I even backed Tony Blackburn once!'

At the same time Roger was experimenting with tape for his own amusement, recording guitar pieces and cutting them up; plugging his bass guitar into his sound studio desk to weave strange sound patterns. He didn't, at the time, realise that there was a BBC department where people were doing similar things all the time.

It was Paddy Kingsland who told him about the Radiophonic Workshop. Paddy was a fellow studio manager who had moved to Maida Vale. A chance encounter encouraged Roger to apply for a week's attachment.

> I think that people who come to the Workshop have an instinct for the job and will find their own way. When I first came I was amazed to find them doing all the things I'd been fiddling about with in my own studio; doing more or less the same thing – but properly!

After his first attachment, Roger went on to become a television announcer and when the opportunity came for him to come to the Workshop on a permanent basis he had to take a cut in salary to do so.

Desmond Briscoe recalls visiting Roger's studio late one night:

> 'There he was, crooning to himself whilst playing the piano. After a hard day's work he had made a complete tape of his own songs. I remember Delia Derbyshire was very taken with them. Roger is the sort of man who just quietly gets on with things.'

During his first three-month attachment, Roger had worked with the 'Golden Age' Workshop team, and believes that it was John Baker, Delia Derbyshire and David Cain who set the style in the 'sixties and opened the Workshop to all sorts of work in radio and television. He starts work in the following way:

> When you meet to discuss a commitment you have to listen a lot to what the producer says, then have a look at the film and sit back and think and let things bubble, bubble in your unconscious, and then let them bubble through to your conscious.
>
> You have to say 'I wonder if that sort of pattern of sound would work for that particular sort of shot?' You can only find out by trying it – maybe nine or ten different mixtures before you come

across the one that works. When you play it to the programme producer it just may not work for him – if so, then it's a case of back to the machines. When you have a personal relationship with a producer you get to know how his mind works and can usually come up with what he wants first time around.

Electronic music is a difficult new medium that has grown up over the last ten years or so mainly because of microcircuits and the development of the synthesiser. There are new horizons opening in electronic music that we cannot readily move towards unless we take three months off to study computer technology. At IRCAM, the research centre for electro-acoustics in Paris, they have recognised the difficulty that the composer has when faced with a battery of electronic equipment. Their idea is that there should be creative teams – basically a composer and a technician, working together. Now this may be fine for a research centre, but at the Workshop we are producing sounds and music which are needed next week. Deadlines are tight, and so we work on our own. If we are fortunate, and come up with the right idea, we can do something big and demanding. The Workshop has already had considerable success with its own programmes.

The Workshop is well-known for its 'spacey' sounds and music; its nightmares and inner troubled worlds. But Roger's work for the BBC Natural History Unit in Bristol has brought a different sort of music to the viewer's attention.

His *Wildlife on One* music for *The Mouse's Tale*, narrated by David Attenborough, caused a flurry of excitement on the BBC switchboard as callers wanted to know where they could buy the record. 'It was,' says Limb, 'one of the best received shows of its kind and I had lots of letters about it. It was not radiophonic music of the weird and wonderful variety but just a jolly little composition almost like a silent movie. About three minutes long, it accompanied the programme's sequence of house mice scampering about.

I was using electronic sounds in a particularly rhythmic way. This is where the satisfaction comes in: to see your music add a whole new dimension, to watch something going out on television and hearing your music playing and say 'Yes, that *really* worked, that really did what I wanted it to do!'

When things like that happen it makes you more certain that the Workshop will never become a factory, as some people have feared. It has a long tradition of experimentation, and we all try to do new things as much as we can. I certainly set aside a bit of time each week when I try to do something that I've never done before: on the Fairlight, for example, I could happily spend three months finding out all it is capable of doing.

*Top right:* Roger Limb adding another dent to the Giants of Steam cylinder. Even in 1982 concrete sources are still a valuable part of the sound palette

*Bottom right:* Roger Limb in Studio E in 1982

I personally don't place too much credence on the expression 'sounds that have not been heard before'. It's just mixing up the ingredients in a different sort of way, in a different sort of setting. I came to electronic music from studying music at university, and I apply what I learned there – harmony, counterpoint and that sort of thing, but the actual work in signature tunes owes as much to jazz and pop as to more formal education.

I arrived at the Workshop at the end of the tape manipulation era and at the beginning of the synthesiser age. The trouble with the future is that you never know about it until you've passed it. . . .

## The man who almost *became* The Body in Question
### *Peter Howell (1974–to date)*

It's not often that the BBC's switchboard is jammed after a programme with people calling up to ask where they can buy the music. It is even rarer for music made at the Radiophonic Workshop to create such an immediate – and lasting – appeal. The callers rang incessantly for two days after a programme in Jonathan Miller's television series *The Body in Question*. The music in question was by Peter Howell, yet another of the staff at Maida Vale who compose without formal training.

Peter Howell

Born in Hove, Brighton, Peter's first interest in music was through Cliff Richard's backing group The Shadows. When he first bought himself a guitar and taught himself to play, it was The Shadows that he wanted to emulate. When he had eventually worked himself up to playing lead guitar with his own group, their repertoire consisted mainly of Shadows numbers.

For eighteen months Peter studied law at Brighton College, continuing his music outside his classes, until he found that he could compose tunes himself and didn't have to rely on what The Shadows had produced before. Not that he could actually write down the notes, but he could – when the mood was right – play spontaneously and create new music. He started 'fiddling about' with tape-recorders and added playing the piano to his music accomplishments.

The possibilities afforded by tape-recorders intrigued him. Having given up law, he joined Glyndebourne Opera in the lighting loft, and then, because of his interest in tape-recording, became an assistant stage manager working with sound. He stayed at Glyndebourne for four years and then joined the BBC, working as a sound recordist covering news events by day and by night. 'It was then,' says Peter, 'that I gained my first awareness of the importance of meeting deadlines.'

As a studio manager in radio he approached the Workshop for an attachment and felt at home from the start. He discovered the same home truth as many before him: that there is all the difference in the world between making electronic music in an amateur way, purely for pleasure, and facing up to the professional problems and deadlines. Paddy Kingsland helped Peter overcome the troublesome technicalities that got in the way of his early compositions. If The Shadows were Peter's first important influence, then Paddy was the second.

'The whole history of the Workshop is so nourishing,' says Peter. 'It has been involved in producing so many influential programmes that the pooled knowledge is absolutely enormous. Though people may come and go, even the people that have gone have never truly gone because they have left their contributions and influences behind them for others to discover.'

Peter's work on *The Body in Question* lasted for fourteen months and resulted in two and three-quarter hours of music. It was the most ambitious project he had ever tackled, and required music for 130 separate 'cues'. Peter's working relationship with the series producer Patrick Uden resulted in such a close understanding of the requirements that out of those 130 cues, only two didn't work first time around.

*The Body in Question* was principally a documentary of a personal nature, drawn from Jonathan Miller's viewpoint. It was not a journey-to-the-centre-of-the-body or anything that would need dramatic feature-film type music. Instead, the radiophonic composer needed to steer a middle course, keeping the viewers interested without making it into a travelogue.

> I do not have a set way of tackling a programme, I just soak up the psychological vibes going around the production and blow in the wind until I find myself going in one direction or the other.

By the end of the series *The Body in Question*, Peter realised that the 'forced learning' of discovering just what worked electronically and what did not, had taught him musically in fourteen months as much as he had learned in his life before.

> Jonathan Miller himself was a very interested and interesting musicologist but he never imposed his own ideas on my compositions. He did suggest that I might think of Purcell or Palestrina or somebody like that as a starting point for the Greenwich Chorus and it was such a good idea that I took it up.

The Greenwich Chorus was an embarrassment, not only to the overloaded BBC switchboard but also to Peter himself. 'The producer liked the piece so much that he used it four or five times over the weeks, and finally it overshadowed the title music.'

Peter describes the Greenwich Chorus as 'quasi-choral, with a bit of the Dalek voice in it'. He put to use his training as a chorister by mouthing vowels and consonants into a Vocoder, a piece of voice-altering equipment that Malcolm Clarke had previously used to good effect in his award-winning programme *August 2026*.

The Vocoder is not normally man's best friend, says Peter. It will only do 60% of what you want it to do, and generally comes out sounding like Sparky's magic piano. I managed to make it sound quite elegant.

Composing is a very selfish thing really; it's self-experimentation throughout because you can't just sit down at a piano and be certain that any chord will have a specific effect. Unless I get the necessary gut reaction then it's not good enough and I try something else. Different approaches are needed for radio and for television. If you are dealing solely in radio, you might also have signposting going with your music – what the actors are saying, ambulance sirens or whatever, all things which would point the listener in the right direction. In television you have a picture in front of you that you can counterpoint with your music.

When you're working from scratch, there's nothing worse than having the whole universe to choose from. It's nice for someone to tell me that my music has definitely got to fit that picture, which lasts exactly one minute five seconds, and that my music must evoke the response that the picture is aiming to achieve. You know where you are, and can get on and do it.

Every job which comes along brings with it its own ideal solution. The Workshop's Organiser, Brian Hodgson, knows from experience which of us is most likely to find that solution. Jobs that are ambiguous and ambivalent right from the start are the worst. You are immediately at risk of going down the wrong path and then being at a psychological disadvantage.

Like all Radiophonic Workshop composers, Peter believes in replying personally to anyone who is sufficiently interested to write in and ask how a particular piece was realised. When a listener from Wembley asked him how he made a piece called *Fancy Fish*, he replied:

The opening and closing was played on a programmed computer musical instrument. This instrument – the Fairlight CMI – is capable of sampling short real sounds and altering and manipulating them to form new instrumental textures. The basic sounds used on *Fancy Fish* were created by

a) rubbing a finger around the rim of a wineglass
b) a chime bar with vibrato and slow attack
c) bubbles created by dropping an aspirin into a glass of water
d) a bass version of c)

The piece was realised totally in the computer without recourse to tape until the final mixdown.

Peter is a keen fan of the Fairlight and has already built up a battery of composite sounds, and named them according to their components. Clarjang is made from a clarinet sound combined with a metallic jangle. Pluckvox combines the plucking of a mandolin note with the second half, his own voice. A vast library of such sounds can be built up and stored on floppy discs. But with so many options and so many unusual sounds available, Peter wonders whether radiophonic composers are not in danger of 'creating licorice-allsorts music'. To guard against this, he tends 'to home in on ten or twelve sounds for each piece I create'.

He is also convinced that current technological advances have made the Workshop a more exciting place to be now than in the past. 'With just the Fairlight there are apparently no limits. The road goes on for ever'. . . .

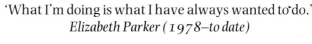

'What I'm doing is what I have always wanted to do.'
*Elizabeth Parker (1978–to date)*

Desmond Briscoe: Elizabeth Parker came to the workshop for a week, as many do, and it was obvious that she was going to stay. Following a post-graduate course on electronic music and acoustics at East Anglia, she came to the BBC as a studio manager and joined the Workshop permanently in January 1978.

Elizabeth Parker

She took over *Blake's Seven* from Richard Yeoman-Clark and went on to produce effects and special sounds for the series for two-and-a-half years.

Elizabeth is unique in the Workshop in that she makes whatever studio she is working in smaller by building a sort of nest and drawing all her equipment around her. She left the Workshop to have her first baby – and came back. Then later she had her second baby knowing that she had been given one of the plum assignments of all time to work on when she came back: David Attenborough's *Living Planet*.

Slim, vivacious and positive, with a great capacity for hard work, she is a very well-organised lady and a very able musician, playing piano and cello.

Says Elizabeth: I always wanted to choose the music that goes behind programmes; it was my ambition ever since I was eleven. For me, the idea of enhancing something – possibly without people knowing it – was enormously appealing. If I had not been lucky enough to come to the Workshop I suppose I would have gone into advertising, a profession that also uses sound in very subtle ways.

My taste in music was always slightly off-beat even though I was formally trained. I have always been interested in sound montage and that has coloured my whole appreciation of music and way of working.

I do an awful lot of work at the planning stage. When I was at home waiting for my baby, I worked quite happily with a tape-recorder and paper with all the time code numbers marked up – that's how I begin. What I like best is making interesting textured sounds by a combination of electronic sources and tape manipulation: like mixing all the wonderful things that a Fairlight allows you to do with only a few old-fashioned loops of tape going round.

You can get an enormous variety of sounds from a synthesiser, but you are limited to a certain extent because they are all electronic sounds.

I get completely wrapped up in my work when I am composing. The time just disappears and I sit there and finish what I set myself to do and completely forget about anything else. I'll work all the hours I possibly can when there's a rush on. Usually things calm down again, and I find myself just hanging around waiting for the graphics to arrive, or whatever else it is that is holding things up.

I did my pilot for *Living Planet* in May 1981 and now, at last, film is coming through to me, even though it is only the 'first-cut' and I have to work from the 'final-cut'. Now I'm able to look at the film and discuss with the executive producer what the pictures suggest to me.

1983 is obviously going to be a very busy year, and I guess it will escalate towards the end, and I might well be working nineteen hours a day. But I'm looking forward to it immensely. After all, I'm lucky in that what I'm doing is what I have always wanted to do.

'If I get the job, when do I start?'
*Jonathan Gibbs (1983 to date)*

Jonathan Gibbs, educated at Cambridge, joined the BBC as a studio manager and is the latest recruit to the permanent staff of the Radiophonic Workshop. Following an earlier attachment, he was invited on a second attachment to cover Elizabeth Parker's absence on maternity leave; he made good use of his time, composing and realising music for the series *Tales from the South China Seas*. He joined the department in January 1983 amidst a positive welter of critical acclaim for his highly evocative 'Indonesian' radiophonic music.

Jonathan Gibbs

# CHAPTER 8
## *Doctor Who*

'There's a children's science fiction serial that's
going to run for six weeks. Can you do a signature tune?'
*Verity Lambert, Producer*

'There's a children's science fiction serial that's going to run for six weeks. Can you do a signature tune?'

Verity Lambert was the first producer of *Doctor Who*, and that short phone query to Desmond Briscoe in 1963 was the start of a collaboration which was destined to continue for considerably longer than six weeks. Twenty years later the intrepid Doctor is still adventuring through time and space and the Workshop is more involved than ever since they now provide all the incidental music as well as special sound effects.

During these years the men and women of Maida Vale have provided so much aural material for the series that reels of tape occupy one entire side of Dick Mills' Workshop studio. Though the good Doctor himself has gone through five incarnations in the very different persons of William Hartnell, Patrick Troughton, Jon Pertwee, Tom Baker and currently Peter Davison each episode has always been preceded by the familiar swooping title music, and every time that the Tardis takes off for yet another extraterrestrial destination it does so with the same laboured lurching sound.

The serial has now taken on epic quality, with a very active Appreciation Society producing literature, an annual handbook and conventions. Workshop staff in particular are linked closely with the programme and are in great demand to talk to fans.

Following her first call, to which Desmond Briscoe had replied, 'Yes, of course we can do your signature tune. Let's get together and talk about it,' Verity Lambert came to the Workshop and explained that not only did she want radiophonic music, something with a beat and something different, but she would really like it to be written by Ron Grainer, one of the most successful television composers of the time. She had also seen and heard a French group called 'Les Structures Sonores' who played glass rods mounted in steel. The sound they made was certainly different, but when she had discussed the possibility of asking them to perform, the Head of TV Music, Lionel Salter, had advised: 'Before you go to Paris, go to Maida Vale and talk to Desmond Briscoe.'

Grainer, who had just finished working with the unit on a programme about railways called *Giants of Steam*, was also known to book the best wind players in London and give them bottles to blow across. Desmond rang him immediately and the collaboration was agreed there and then.

Delia Derbyshire was the Workshop composer who took over from there: 'Ron had worked his tune very carefully to fit in with the graphics which had been done by a technique which was very new and unusual for those days – camera feedback. He used delightful expressions for the sort of noises he wanted: "windbubble and clouds" – things like that.'

Brian Hodgson recollects: 'We were all very impressed by the sounds made by Les Structures Sonores, who had appeared on the BBC TV Arts programme *Monitor*. But whereas they made new sounds on glass rods set in steel, we used sine and square wave generators, a white noise generator and a special beat frequency generator. We then cut, shaped, filtered and manipulated them in various ways until finally the separate tracks were ready for mixing and synchronisation.'

Delia Derbyshire explains: 'Each one of the swoops you hear is a carefully-timed handswoop on the oscillators. The swoops were then put together very carefully so that you cannot hear the joins.' The *Doctor Who* theme meant instant public awareness for the Workshop; it was probably the biggest boost the place had ever had. As the series grew more popular and viewers multiplied, the BBC Radiophonic Workshop became a household name and for the staff at Maida Vale *Doctor Who* was both a milestone and a millstone. Certainly the signature tune engendered an interest and loyalty that still runs strong twenty years later.

Dick Mills: Since then whenever we've had a new series of *Doctor Who* someone has said: 'Wouldn't it be nice to up-date the signature tune'; and every time there's been such an outcry – not necessarily from people in authority but from the people who are actually working on the show – we tended to compromise and just do a cosmetic change. But then, a couple of years ago, Peter Howell tackled a much more radical contemporary up-date.

Peter Howell: I realised how dangerous an area I was entering because the tune was so very well established and in a way had helped make the Workshop's name for all of us. The Doctor Who Appreciation Society are very, very efficient and they *do* chase people. I didn't want to throw out the baby with the bathwater; didn't want to do something so ridiculously new that nobody would know it was the same tune. As far as I was concerned, I was trying to prove that you could use all the techniques that we have learned over the years and still make something fresh with all this new equipment.

This was in the eighteenth season of *Doctor Who* and I was slightly fearful not only of altering the theme and being too sacrilegious in the eyes of the die-hard *Doctor Who* fans, but also of being commissioned to write the incidental music as well. Not that I didn't want to do it – it was just the time factor that was the problem.

The programme producer, John Nathan-Turner, had decided that since his futuristic sci-fi series needed equally futuristic sci-fi incidental music that was best provided by electronic and synthesiser sound quality, the Workshop must become involved. Once he had produced the new-look signature tune and the heavens had not opened and swallowed him up, Peter Howell pushed his luck a little further and used the theme as continuity wherever he thought it helped.

He also produced another Workshop 'realisation' of someone else's tune, this time for the Doctor's mechanical dog K9. An outside composer had provided a K9 theme whose 'saucy' quality Peter Howell so liked that he used it with his music for the *K9 and Company* show.

K9, the dog-like walking/talking computer

The incidental music that the Workshop was now producing for the series excited the television production team. It fitted their requirements so well that from now on music would become a more important *Doctor Who* ingredient than it ever had been previously.

From April 1981 until February 1983, ten *Doctor Who* stories had incidental music by the following workshop composers:

*Fort to Doomsday* – Roger Limb     *Earthshock* – Malcolm Clarke
*The Visitation* – Paddy Kingsland     *Timeflight* – Roger Limb
*Kinda* – Peter Howell     *Snakedance* – Peter Howell
*Castravalva* – Paddy Kingsland     *Ark of Infinity* – Roger Limb
*Black Orchid* – Roger Limb     *The King's Demons* – Peter Howell

As Howell had feared, his 'up-date' of the *Doctor Who* signature tune pleased some, but not all. Right from the start, the theme music was always controversial.

'My son loves the programme, but as soon as the music is played he goes rigid and deathly white and is terrified', wrote one concerned mother to *Radio Times* in 1973. Barry Letts, who was then producing, couldn't offer that much help. 'Over the years there have been many similar reports of children being frightened both by the music and the stories,' he said.

The new-style signature tune proved 'a poor substitute' to some, and a 'modernisation worthy of congratulations' to others.

In the time scale of the Doctor, who keeps a 500-year Diary, this was trivial and transitory stuff. What had survived almost without change since the very early days were two basic sounds: The Tardis take-off and the voices of those pepper-pot foes, the Daleks.

The man responsible for devising both was Brian Hodgson.

The Tardis take-off was quite a problem at first and I had to think about it a lot before I knew where I was going. I remember sitting in the Kensington Odeon watching the movie *Exodus* when the answer came to me in a mental breakthrough. I drew it out and it was a great big shape of things going in two directions at once, so that things which were coming down were also going away from you. It was quite a structured piece and later on when I was asked to rewrite it for a record when the original notation had long been lost, I found it quite easy to do.

Having decided on the sound that he wanted to achieve, Brian then had to realise it. He derived the basic sound by strumming his front door key against the open strings of the Workshop's gutted piano, and the final result was achieved by a great deal of tape treatment. Though he bent his key, it was obviously well worthwhile, since visitors to the Workshop today still touch the piano and feel they are touching television history.

Brian Hodgson about to strike a chord on the original piano utilised for the *Doctor Who* Tardis take-off

When scriptwriter Terry Nation invented the Daleks, the problem was not that they would ever ex-ter-min-ate the series but would very soon take it over. Their success was immediate and not only for the way they looked. 'You know when you have achieved something successful when children in the street imitate it,' says Brian. 'Even though we were happy with the result, we never imagined just how much of an impact it would make.'

The Daleks were originally said to have been named from the DA to LEK sections of an encyclopaedia. Their voices were the direct descendants of an otherwise forgettable robot called Jones, who appeared originally in a BBC children's programme, *Sword from the Stars*.

Brian Hodgson: The Jones Robot was a very domesticated sort of robot and had an ordinary sort of voice, modulated at 30 cycles. When we came to do the Daleks we remembered the Jones Robot and combined him with the incredibly brilliant characterisation given to the voice by actor Peter Hawkins. Peter's voice was switched on and off electrically 30 times a second – and the Daleks spoke for the very first time! At first we were much concerned whether the Dalek voice would prove too grating and unpleasant for the children – even children who by now were used to big sounds. We soon realised we had no need for worry, they took to the sound immediately.

Desmond Briscoe: 'It is almost impossible to destroy the essential sound quality of the human voice. The power of communication is the bit you have to worry about.'

Later on, Brian went on from the Daleks to the Mechanoids and treated them a little more roughly, smashing up their voices to fragments, putting bits of them back together again, adding a continuous note and speeding up the whole thing.

The Daleks were – and still are – enormously popular with viewers. But not all the sounds that the Workshop has made for the series have been well received. There are some noises to which even the most dedicated *Doctor Who* fan just cannot relate. Some very high-pitched noises which Brian made for a type of large ant featured in a story called *The Zarbies* brought an avalanche of complaints which rather took him by surprise: 'I had thought that anything pitched in such a way that the sound could be transmitted over television couldn't possibly be high enough to be unpleasant.'

Over the years many monsters have been made vocal by the Workshop. Some, like a Mechanoid, came with a description of just what he looked like and it was left to the Workshop to work out how he sounded. Others, like the Cybermen, were a lot of trouble.

We weren't fond of them at all, says Brian. Dick Mills and I tried all

*Left:* The Daleks have landed in London . . .

*Inset:* Tom Baker as Doctor Who at the control desk as the Tardis takes off sorts of ways of overcoming the problem of giving them the right kind of voices. At one point we had the actor, Peter Hawkins, fitted with a false palate with a loudspeaker inside it.

Peter suffered greatly for the cause because he has such a terrific voice and here we were trying every sort of different way of altering the marvellous way in which he spoke. The Sensorites were much easier and rather fun because the producer came to us and said: 'Well, the terrible thing is that we've run out of money for scenery, so this story has to be set entirely in the Tardis and all the viewers will see are faces at the window.' So for four weeks Dick and I made noises to go with the faces at the window. Though that may sound flippant, neither Brian nor Dick are anything but serious about the way in which they tackle such commitments. Says Dick Mills: 'The script describes the monster and its effect on people. We've got to make the monster sound exactly right. A challenge is always a challenge.'

Not all monsters need the vocal abilities of a Mechanoid or a Cybermen. Some of them just roar at people, like the Yeti or slobber like the Slyther.

The Cybermen are back . . .

Working closely with the programme for the best part of ten years was an enjoyable experience for Brian, though he finally decided he had had enough and passed the mantle to Dick Mills. Dick Mills has assisted with *Doctor Who* right from the inception of the series, and took over the job when Brian Hodgson left to form his own company.

It was not at all like sliding into an already warm seat: more like being plunged in at the deep end. One day I wasn't doing it and the next day I was – faced with a synthesiser as big as the room and Dudley Simpson, the composer who had successfully collaborated with Brian over the years.

Dudley naturally assumed that I would take over where Brian had left off, knowing everything there was to know about helping composers. What we had to do first was to find a common language. On the first day I discovered that Dudley was fond of 'low trajectory noises' which worried me more than somewhat since I didn't know what they sounded like. We're still trying to work out what he meant but since Brian had provided them before me, I did too and there were no complaints.

Malcolm Clarke in 1982 mixing down one of his tracks of incidental music for the Doctor's latest Cyberman adventure

We worked very well together, Dudley and I, and walked a bit further down the path of exploration together. The trouble with the path of exploration is that it is always longer than the time they give you to walk down it. These days I work from a videotape of the completed and edited recording, rather than make the effects after reading the script. Each twenty-five-minute episode comes to us so that we can discuss with the director what parts of the action need sounds, and which need to be strengthened with music.

The first decision is whether to use natural sound – and that means anything that can be recorded with a microphone – or whether I go straightway to a small electronic synthesiser. When I've made my mind up about the sounds and sound qualities then I have perhaps a week to produce all the sounds before the final dubbing session at Television Centre when all the components are put onto the one master tape for transmission. That session lasts all day for one *Doctor Who* episode.

I have positively enjoyed making many of the sounds for the programme over the years. When Brian and I came to put together an LP for BBC Records, *Doctor Who Sound Effects*, we found that we were able to visit seven alien worlds as well as encountering extraterrestrial occurrences on earth.

Probably my favourite *Doctor Who* sound of all came when one of the Doctor's heroines was being threatened by something indescribably nasty. It didn't so much roar as squelch. I used handfuls of the green goo jelly stuff that mechanics use to get grease off their hands after repairing a car. The splodgy squelching sounds were very satisfying but the stuff was hard to handle – it kept getting out of control and squirting everywhere. I had a very messy shirtfront and microphone after that session.

Monsters of one sort and another have been Dick's constant companions ever since he first came to Maida Vale. Quite apart from the monsters encountered by *Doctor Who*, there seems to be a regular Workshop trade in dinosaurs, plesiosaurs and other prehistoric monsters.

It's all very understandable. There is no way that programme producers can go out and record them at London Zoo, and those at the Natural History Museum in South Kensington don't say very much these days. So the producers come to me and I growl and roar all day and go home with a sore throat.

The most important thing is to get the size right. Everyone knows that a prehistoric monster tends to be on the large size, but when a script mentions a new monster for *Doctor Who* I like to go along to Television Centre and see it in the flesh, so to speak, and compare it to the physical size of the actors and the sets. Then I can use the correct sound scale for something five times the size of a house and not produce the smaller sounds I might make for a clockwork robot.

On the other hand, things can be contracted in size; for instance, there was a time when the Doctor was injected into his own brain. Words in a script are not the same as the actual visuals that will appear on the screen, and it helps to have a sense of scale.

Dick considers voices to be of crucial importance, whether for monsters, robots or even animals. Sometimes it is imperative that the actor's voice be heavily treated radiophonically; other times the actor's delivery is vital.

The Daleks just wouldn't be Daleks unless they had the monotonous flat delivery which we then chop into little bits. When people ring up and ask me how to make a Dalek voice then I tell them: 'With a ring modulator and a 30-cycle square wave.' Then they go away and try it, but it doesn't sound anything like a Dalek because the dispassionate, unfeeling delivery just isn't there.

Like other members of the Workshop who work on *Doctor Who*, Dick often finds himself face to face with his fans at the various *Doctor Who* meetings and conventions that are held around the country from time to time.

Knowing the subject thoroughly helps a lot, and Dick can point to a whole wall of his studio lined with tape boxes of sounds from *Doctor*

Part of the *Doctor Who* sound collection which now numbers over 200 tapes

*Who* stories going back to the first episodes of all. This *Doctor Who* archive is particularly useful since, when the Doctor comes to revisit a location that he has been to before, there is reference available to help. Whether it is background noises on an alien planet, or weaponry used by a particular band of adversaries, there would be someone watching who would write in to complain if it proved inconsistent. 'It is very nice to know that even after twenty years someone is keeping track of continuity out there,' says Dick.

Though everyone connected with the making of *Doctor Who* takes it very seriously indeed, Dick remembers one incident when Tom Baker brought a sense of humour into a sequence which enabled Dick to go overboard on his sounds.

Tom was different from the preceding Doctors in a number of ways, and did things that no one else had done. For instance, he would look straight at the camera and play to the audience. In this particular episode, here was the Doctor in a very serious situation indeed. The console of the Tardis had just gone wrong, and he was struggling with the controls, anxiously hurrying away from goodness knows what danger outside. But nothing would work. Down he went under the console with two bits of wire that he hoped would get the Tardis off the ground and everyone aboard to safety.

He gave a knowing look at the audience, and went off with the wires. Would they work? No – they didn't! The whole Tardis control blew up and fell apart with a great clatter of tin cans and horrible twanging noises. It was a moment of light relief that we all enjoyed, but I wouldn't dare hope for another such comedy sound routine in light years.

The five faces of *Doctor Who*:
(from left to right)
William Hartnell
Patrick Troughton
Jon Pertwee
Tom Baker
Peter Davison

# CHAPTER 9
## *Permutated Poets*

'Voices and sounds that loomed, struck, tottered
out of darkness . . .'
*Peter Vansittart writing about* The Origins of Capital
and The Descent of Power

Five years to the day after the Workshop first opened, *The Listener* noted
the fact that:

> Quietly and without much publicity, in fact, a new art seems to
> have grown up, an art which is particularly suited to what is
> nowadays frequently regarded as the 'old-fashioned' medium of
> sound radio. It is an art which is allied to music – these techniques
> of manipulating sound are used by composers of electronic music
> and *musique concrète*. Indeed with such compositions it is often
> difficult to say where the work of the composer ends and that of the
> technician begins. Music of this kind is rapidly becoming familiar
> on the Continent, though little of it is yet composed here and even
> some reputable critics do not seem to appreciate the difference
> between the various kinds of artificially created sound. *Musique
> concrète* uses the ordinary sounds of everyday life, while electronic
> music, as its name implies, is created purely by electronic devices;
> a workshop like the BBC's can manipulate all these ingredients, as
> well as musical instruments and any other source of sound it cares
> to use, to create its original soundtracks.

The article was sparked off by a series of four programmes by writer
Barry Bermange entitled *Inventions for Radio* – a collaboration between
one man and 'the ingenious new technical effects known as
radiophonics.' (In fact, these were done by one woman, Delia
Derbyshire.)

The programmes were well received by the public, and critics praised
the Workshop's unexpected discretion: 'The monster is being tamed,'
said one newspaper.

> Putting it at its simplest, the technique of these programmes is to
> mix fragments of recorded speech about a particular subject – in
> this case, dreams and visions of death and eternity – with an
> artificially produced atmospheric soundtrack. The result, as was

demonstrated in Mr Bermange's previous programmes, *The Dreams* and *Amor Dei*, can be hypnotic. The sound effects, whether suggesting horror, loneliness, or religious exaltations, enhance words which in themselves are often totally banal. And the speakers can be made to seem almost poets or opera singers by editing their words in juxtaposition with each other, or by repeating the same phrases in different keys, at different volumes or different speeds.

Interestingly, the Workshop would, for the next few years, be working closely with poets, sometimes using such techniques.

It was not only composers and creative broadcasters, with their recording machines and tapes, who had discovered 'concrete' sounds. A number of poets were also working in a new and novel way, and calling the visual results 'concrete poetry'. Some performed their work and called themselves 'sound poets'.

It was therefore right and proper that so many of them found their way to the Radiophonic Workshop, introduced either by the BBC poetry producer George MacBeth, himself a poet, or by Douglas Cleverdon and other programme producers.

One of the leaders of the international movement was the Austrian poet Ernst Jandl, who had been outstandingly influential in popularising the new poetry to an audience of six thousand in the Royal Albert Hall.

Jandl came to the Workshop in 1966 to give his own readings and 'orchestrations' of *Laut und Luise*, a programme that employed all the resources of the Workshop in adding the right radiophonic background.

A number of radiophonic techniques, including the speeding up and slowing down of tapes, multiple recording, and echo and feedback were used to match the poet's intellectual subtlety, musical ingenuity, vigour and humour.

Whilst composers of *musique concrète* had been using the technique of cutting up recording tape since the earliest days, it was only around 1960 that the idea spread to literature. William Burroughs pioneered and popularised it in his novel *The Naked Lunch*, but it was introduced to him by a fellow American poet and painter, Brion Gysin.

Burroughs and Gysin collaborated (with Sinclair Beiles and Gregory Corso) on a pamphlet entitled *Minutes to Go* (1960) which contained their first cut-ups and also Gysin's 'permutated poems', based on the geometric progression $5 \times 4 \times 3 \times 2 \times 1$ and resulting in every line carrying a contradictory message. Nothing remotely like it had ever been seen on the printed page before and Douglas Cleverdon speedily invited Gysin to record his poems with a background of radiophonic sound.

Brion Gysin

Gysin's delivery of such lines as *I am That I am, Rub Out The Words, Junk Is No Good Baby* – exploring all potential sounds and meanings of the words – was so powerful that technicians were left in awe at the end of his 'performance'. Gysin treated the Workshop's battery of tape-recorders as performers in their own right. 'Let the machines speak,' he exhorted. 'Even if they go wrong, they are still saying something.'

A typical permutated poem, *I am that I am* is printed opposite.

The public and critics generally considered the marriage of concrete music, concrete sound and concrete poetry as avant-garde, distinctly odd – but definitely interesting. *The Listener* reviewer greeted such experimental programmes as 'manna from heaven'.

'Dotty and refreshing' was the verdict of another critic on Bob Cobbing's *ABC of Sound*, made at the Workshop as an experiment in concrete poetry.

Bob Cobbing

The programme put to the test the first principles of radio: communication by means of sound. Cobbing read his alphabet – an extensive montage of carefully chosen words in various languages – which the Workshop then speeded up, slowed down, dilated, distended, condensed and otherwise deformed.

Dick Mills remembers it as 'very much an inspired programme . . . with a tartan background being woven by the Workshop while Cobbing recited all the Ms – Macpherson, MacFarlane, etc., to a treated vocal skirling of bagpipes and similarly heathery sounds'.

The *Radio Times* noted that it was a programme 'to develop an art of pure sound'. The *Guardian* critic Anne Duchene wrote: 'The Alphabet, in whatever interpretation, made unexpectedly invigorating radio, and was an experiment which should be repeated (though it is not apparently scheduled for such, suggesting that even by Third Programme standards it rates as very experimental indeed).'

None of the staff then in residence can have easily forgotten the visit to Maida Vale by poet and novelist Rosemary Tonks who came to the unit to make her programme and then subsequently wrote a novel called *The Bloater*, in which – the staff are convinced – they appear with individual characteristics which have been applied to different bodies.

However true that may be, the programme *Sono-Montage*, broadcast in June 1966, was very definitely an experimental production which was approved by *The Listener* reviewer Kevin Crossley-Holland. 'Experimental programmes are so few and far between . . . and *Sono-Montage* must have been the end-product of much hard work. If it was not entirely satisfying, it was exceedingly stimulating, even if it did call for a glass of brandy, or a warm bath, afterwards.'

Some of the poets were trying to find an answer to the age-old question: when does sound become music? Lily Greenham came in April 1975 with an extraordinary work entitled *Relativity*.

```
I AM THAT I AM      AM I AM THAT I      I AM I AM THAT      THAT I AM I AM      AM THAT I AM I
AM THAT I AM        AM AM I THAT I      I AM I THAT AM      THAT I AM I AM      I THAT I AM AM
I THAT I AM AM      AM I THAT AM I      I AM I THAT AM      AM I AM I THAT      I AM I AM AM
THAT I AM I AM      AM THAT I AM        I AM THAT AM I      I I AM THAT AM      THAT I I AM AM
AM THAT I I AM      AM THAT AM I I      I AM THAT AM        I AM THAT AM        THAT I I AM AM
THAT AM I I AM      AM I AM THAT I      THAT AM I AM        I AM THAT AM        AM I I AM THAT
I AM I THAT AM      AM I I AM THAT      THAT AM I AM        I THAT AM AM I      I AM THAT I
AM I I THAT AM      AM AM I I THAT      THAT AM AM I I      I AM THAT AM I      I I THAT AM AM
I I AM THAT AM      AM I I AM THAT      THAT AM I I AM      AM THAT AM I I      I AM THAT AM I
AM I THAT AM        AM AM I I THAT      THAT AM I I AM      AM THAT AM I        I I THAT AM AM
I AM I THAT AM      AM I AM I THAT      THAT AM I I AM      I THAT AM AM I      I AM THAT AM I
THAT I AM I AM      AM THAT I AM        AM AM I THAT I      I AM I THAT         I AM AM I
I I THAT I AM AM    AM THAT I AM        AM AM THAT I        THAT AM AM I        I I THAT AM AM
I I THAT AM AM      AM I I THAT AM      AM AM I I THAT      THAT AM AM I        I THAT AM AM I
THAT I AM AM        AM THAT I I AM      AM AM THAT I I      I AM AM THAT        I I AM AM THAT
I THAT I AM AM      AM I THAT I AM      AM AM I THAT        I AM AM THAT        THAT I I AM AM
AM THAT I I AM      I AM THAT I         I AM THAT I AM      I I AM I AM THAT    AM I I AM
THAT AM I I AM      AM AM THAT I I      I AM I AM THAT      THAT I AM I AM      I THAT I AM I
AM I THAT I AM      AM I AM THAT I      I AM I AM THAT      AM I AM I THAT      I THAT I AM I
I AM THAT I AM      AM THAT I AM        I AM I THAT AM      THAT I AM I AM      AM I AM I
THAT I AM AM        AM I THAT AM I      I AM I THAT AM      AM I AM I THAT      THAT AM I AM I
I THAT AM I AM      I I AM THAT AM      I AM I THAT AM      THAT I AM AM        AM THAT AM I
I AM THAT AM I      I AM I THAT AM      I AM THAT AM I      AM I AM THAT        AM THAT AM I
THAT I AM I AM      I THAT I AM AM      AM I AM I THAT      AM I I THAT         THAT I AM I
AM THAT I AM I      I AM THAT I AM      AM I AM THAT I      I AM AM I THAT      THAT I AM I
I AM AM THAT I      I I AM AM THAT      THAT I I AM AM      AM THAT I I AM      AM AM THAT I
AM I AM THAT I      I AM I AM THAT      THAT I I AM AM      AM THAT I I AM      AM AM THAT I
I AM AM THAT I      I AM I AM THAT      THAT I I AM AM      AM THAT I I AM      AM AM THAT I
I AM THAT I AM      I AM AM I THAT      THAT I AM AM        AM I AM I THAT      AM I THAT I
AM I THAT I AM      I AM AM I THAT      THAT I AM AM        AM I AM THAT        AM I THAT I
I THAT AM I AM      I I THAT AM AM      AM I THAT AM        AM AM I THAT        THAT AM AM I
THAT I AM AM        I THAT I AM AM      AM I THAT AM        AM I THAT AM        I AM AM THAT
I AM THAT I AM      I AM I THAT AM      AM I AM THAT        THAT AM I AM I      AM I THAT AM
THAT AM I AM        I THAT I AM AM      AM I AM THAT        I AM THAT AM        THAT I AM I
AM THAT I AM        I AM THAT I AM      AM I AM THAT        I AM I THAT         THAT I AM I
AM I THAT I AM      I THAT I AM AM      I I THAT AM AM      AM I I AM THAT      AM I THAT I
THAT AM I I AM      I THAT AM I AM      I I THAT AM AM      I I I THAT AM AM    AM THAT I I
AM AM THAT I I      I AM AM THAT I      I I AM AM THAT      I I THAT AM AM      THAT AM I I
AM AM I I THAT      I THAT AM I AM      I AM AM THAT        THAT I I AM AM      AM AM I I THAT
THAT AM AM I I      I AM THAT I AM      I I AM THAT        I I AM I THAT       AM AM I I THAT
I AM I AM THAT      THAT I AM I AM      AM THAT I AM I      I AM THAT I AM      I I AM THAT I
AM I I AM THAT      THAT AM I I AM      AM THAT I I AM      AM AM THAT I I      I I AM THAT I
I I AM AM THAT      THAT I I AM AM      AM AM THAT I I      AM AM THAT I I      I I AM THAT I
AM I AM I THAT      THAT AM I AM        AM THAT I AM I      THAT I AM I        I I AM THAT I
I AM AM I THAT      THAT I AM I AM      AM THAT I AM I      I AM THAT I AM      AM AM I THAT I
AM I AM I THAT      THAT AM I AM        I THAT AM I AM      AM I I THAT         AM I THAT I
I AM AM I THAT      THAT AM I AM        I THAT AM I AM      AM I THAT AM        AM I THAT I
AM AM I I THAT      THAT AM AM I I      I THAT AM I AM      I THAT AM I        I I THAT AM
                                                                              1150
                                                                              1160
                                                                              1170
                                                                              1180
                                                                              1190
                                                                              1200
```

```
I I AM AM THAT      THAT I I AM AM      AM THAT I I AM      AM AM THAT I I      I AM AM THAT I
I I AM AM THAT      THAT I I AM AM      AM THAT I I AM      AM AM THAT I I      I AM AM THAT I
I I AM AM THAT      THAT I AM I AM      AM THAT I AM I      I AM THAT I AM      AM I AM THAT I
AM I I AM THAT      THAT AM I AM        AM THAT AM I        I AM THAT I AM      I I AM THAT AM
I AM I AM THAT      THAT I AM I AM      I AM THAT AM        I AM THAT I AM      I I AM THAT AM
AM I I AM THAT      THAT I AM I AM      I AM THAT AM        I AM THAT I AM      I I AM THAT AM
AM I AM I THAT      THAT AM I AM I      I THAT AM I AM      AM I THAT I        I AM I THAT AM
I AM AM I THAT      THAT AM I AM I      I THAT AM I AM      AM I THAT I        AM AM I THAT I
AM AM I I THAT      THAT AM I AM        I THAT AM I        AM I THAT AM        AM I I THAT AM
I AM AM I THAT      THAT AM AM I I      I THAT AM I        I THAT AM AM        AM I I THAT AM
AM AM I I THAT      THAT AM I AM        I THAT AM I        AM I THAT I        I AM I THAT AM
I THAT I AM AM      AM I THAT I AM      I AM AM I THAT      I AM AM THAT       THAT I AM I AM
I I THAT I AM AM    AM THAT I I AM      AM AM THAT I I      I AM AM THAT       I I AM AM THAT
I I THAT AM AM      AM I I THAT AM      AM AM I I THAT      THAT AM AM I       I THAT AM AM
THAT I I AM AM      AM THAT I I AM      AM AM I I THAT      THAT AM AM I I      I I AM AM THAT
I THAT I AM AM      AM I THAT I AM      AM AM I THAT       I AM AM THAT        THAT I AM AM
I THAT I AM AM      AM I THAT I AM      I AM I THAT        THAT AM I AM        THAT I AM I
THAT I AM I AM      AM I THAT I AM      I AM I AM THAT     I AM THAT I         I AM I THAT
I AM THAT I AM      AM I AM THAT I      I AM I AM THAT     THAT I AM I AM      AM THAT I AM
AM I THAT I AM      AM I AM THAT I      I AM THAT AM       THAT I AM I         I THAT I AM AM
THAT AM I I AM      AM THAT AM I I      I AM THAT AM I     I I AM THAT AM      AM I I AM THAT
AM THAT I I AM      AM AM THAT I I      I AM THAT AM       AM THAT AM I        I AM THAT AM I
I I AM THAT AM      AM I I AM THAT      THAT AM I I AM     AM THAT AM I        AM I THAT AM
I AM I THAT AM      AM I AM I THAT      THAT AM I AM       I THAT AM AM        I THAT AM AM
I AM I THAT AM      AM I AM I THAT      THAT AM AM I       I THAT AM AM        I THAT AM AM I
I AM THAT I AM      AM I AM THAT I      THAT AM I AM       I AM THAT AM        I AM AM THAT
THAT AM I AM       AM I THAT I AM      THAT AM I AM       I AM THAT AM        AM I THAT AM
I THAT AM I AM      AM THAT I AM        I AM THAT I AM     I I AM THAT AM      I AM THAT AM
THAT AM I I AM     AM I THAT AM I      I AM THAT I AM     I AM THAT AM        I AM THAT AM
AM THAT I I AM     AM AM THAT I I      I AM THAT AM       AM I AM THAT        THAT AM I AM
I AM THAT I AM     AM I AM THAT I      I AM I THAT AM     AM I AM I THAT      THAT AM I AM
THAT I AM I AM     AM THAT I AM I      I AM THAT AM       THAT I AM I AM      AM I THAT AM
I THAT AM I AM     AM THAT AM I I      I AM THAT AM       I I AM THAT AM      AM AM I THAT
THAT AM I I AM    AM AM THAT I I      I AM AM THAT I      I I AM AM THAT      AM AM I THAT
AM THAT I I AM    AM I THAT AM I      I AM AM THAT I      THAT I I AM AM      AM AM THAT I I
I AM THAT I AM    AM I AM THAT I      I AM AM THAT        AM I I THAT         THAT AM AM I
THAT I AM I AM    AM I AM I THAT      I AM I THAT AM      THAT I I AM AM      AM AM THAT I
AM I THAT I AM    I AM THAT I AM      I AM I AM THAT      AM AM I THAT        AM I THAT AM
I AM THAT I AM    I I THAT I AM AM    I AM I AM THAT      AM AM I THAT        THAT AM I AM
THAT I AM AM      I THAT I AM AM      I AM I THAT AM      THAT I AM I AM      AM I AM THAT
AM THAT AM I I    I AM THAT AM I      I I AM THAT AM      AM AM I I THAT      AM AM I THAT I
AM I THAT AM      I AM AM THAT I      I I AM THAT         THAT I I AM AM      AM I AM I THAT
AM AM THAT I I    I AM AM THAT I      I I AM AM THAT      THAT I I AM AM      AM AM I THAT I
THAT AM AM I I    I THAT AM AM I      I I THAT AM AM      AM I I AM THAT      I AM AM I THAT
AM THAT AM I I    I AM THAT AM I      AM I THAT I        AM AM I THAT         AM AM I THAT I
AM I AM THAT I    I AM THAT I AM      AM I AM THAT I      THAT I AM I         AM I AM I THAT
AM I THAT AM      I AM I THAT AM      AM I THAT AM        I AM THAT AM        THAT AM I AM
AM I THAT AM      I AM I THAT AM      AM I I AM THAT      THAT AM I I AM      I THAT AM I AM
                                                                             1210
                                                                             1220
                                                                             1230
                                                                             1240
                                                                             1250
                                                                             1260
```

```
velOcity     velOcity     velOcity     velOcity      velOcity
    of              of    of     of         of
       nO...    nO...    nO...     nO...     nO...
          bOdy      bOdy      bOdy      bOdy      bOdy
            excEEds excEEds      excEEds      excEEds      excEEds
               the              the      the      the       the
                  velOcity     velOcity      velOcity      velOcity  velOcity
                     of              of    of     of        of
                        lIght     lIght     lIght     lIght      lIght
```

This small sample published in the *Radio Times* was but a fraction of the whole. 'It demonstrates,' said Lily Greenham, 'how a sentence can be given shape and drive in a musical sense beyond its meaning. The term Lingual Music derives from this systematic use of spoken language.'

The excerpts which made up the programme were drawn from Albert Einstein's mass/energy equation and the colours visible in the spectrum of white light. Desmond Briscoe produced the programme, which was intended to be listened to as music rather than poetry. Richard Yeoman-Clark and Peter Howell helped to realise the radiophonic sound.

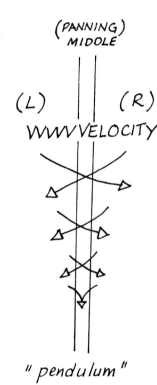

*" pendulum "*

A sound event in time

> I think that everyone who was around the Workshop at the time joined in this one, Desmond Briscoe recalls. Richard Baker and Lily Greenham were the main voices, but we all did our bit. Lily had said in her introductory remarks that although the programme was broadcast in stereo it was possible that some listeners would hear apparent quadrophonic effects. Sounds odd – but a fact.

A strangely haunting programme, *Relativity* was so short (about eight and a half minutes) that it was repeated in the same broadcast with a spoken link. . . . 'The silence you have just heard was the velocity of light' . . . 'Pause' . . . 'Reflection' . . . 'The Second Hearing' – after which the programme began again.

So far the Workshop had encountered inventions for radio (Bermange), permutated poems (Gysin), concrete poetry (Cobbing), lingual music (Greenham).

Whatever next, the composers wondered.

What came next was, in fact, A.R.T.H.U.R.

Described by his creator, the poet Laurence Lerner, as 'a medium-sized digital computer', A.R.T.H.U.R. just happened also to write poetry – or, to be precise, Lerner wrote the poems but in thoughts and opinions proper to such an Automatic Record Tabulator and Heuristically Unreliable Reasoner.

Some of the subjects that A.R.T.H.U.R. wrote about needed appropriately different voices, and Richard Yeoman-Clark, the

Workshop composer assigned to the programme, specified in his hand-written notes just how to produce, radiophonically, the right-sounding voices to be Inventive, Hesitant, Watery, Religious and all the rest.

Notes written by Richard Yeoman-Clark for A.R.T.H.U.R.

The *Radio Times* described the programme as: 'a bout of Arthuritis'. Yeoman-Clark also devised a system of differently coloured underlinings which peppered each poem in order to identify A.R.T.H.U.R.'s different voices or, in some cases, quotes from elsewhere. The result made a very pretty picture on the page. (Symbols have been used here instead of colours.) Might this, we may well be forgiven for asking ourselves, be considered a minor form of concrete art?

What could possibly follow the problems and joys of aiding a poetry-writing computer called A.R.T.H.U.R.?

How about making the sea speak? Or providing a voice for the Loch Ness Monster? Both tasks were tackled by the Workshop, plus another encounter with an imaginary computer, this time stumbling its way to writing a first Christmas card message, and not quite making it:

... 'merry ... merry ... merry ... chrys ... merry chrysanthemum' ...

## Arthur takes a test for divergent thinking

(How many uses can you find for a paper clip?)


It can clip paper,

It can clip papery substances.

It can clip sheets.

It can clip leaves.   Can it clip leaves?

      Yes, Arthur, it can.

It can clip branches.

      No, Arthur, not branches.

It can not clip branches

It can be put down.

It can be picked up.

It can be put down in a heap of paper clips.

It can be put down in a heap of junk.

It can be put down in a heap of dung.

It can be put down a mine      where it could clip paper

                                  clip papery substances

                                  be picked up.

It can be picked up with one hand

               with one finger      that would be a test

               with a magnet

               with a fishing rod

               with the teeth       those would be games

It can be opened out                  that would be wire

Wire could be         a wire hook

                 a wire man

                 a wireless

      No, Arthur, a wireless isn't made of wire.

Wire could not be     a wireless

Wire could be     a telegram

It can clip telegrams.

It can clip letters.

It can clip nails.

      No, Arthur, not nails.

It can not clip nails.

Can it clip hedges?

      No, Arthur, not hedges

It can not not clip hedges.

Can it clip letters?

      Yes, letters.

It can clip A to B

It can clip B to C

It can clip C to

      Arthur, diverge, diverge!

It can clip A to C.

It can unclip A from B

It can be used as a question in a divergence test,

It can clip cli cli cli cli ..........

It could be used to mend mend mend me


1 ═══Arthur's usual voice

2 〰〰Arthur's memory and heuristic processes

     (comes from the depths of the machine)

     thoughtful, receptive, obedient   but still Arthur's voice

3 - - - --Arthur's more inventive, more speculative voice

     (a bit further from human speech)

     more quivering, more metallic

4 ▬▬ Human voice. Untreated, I think.

The poet involved was Edwin Morgan, and the programme was called *The Sound of Edwin Morgan*. It was produced by Desmond Briscoe and realised by Peter Howell.

'Morgan was a very quiet and scholarly person,' recalls Desmond Briscoe, 'but he certainly presented us with some bizarre imaginings.'

*The Loch Ness Monster's Song* provided an opportunity for radiophonic burbling that haunted Desmond Briscoe when he was visiting the Orkneys to make recordings for his programme about another poet, George Mackay Brown: 'I tuned in my hotel radio to hear *Pick of the Week*: and there was our Loch Ness monster burbling away. Then, the following week, it was there again when I listened to *Pick of the Week* introducing that week's programme which contained a *serious* item on Nessie! Orcadians would meet me in the street and say, 'I liked your Loch Ness Monster'; it even achieved a cartoon in *The Scotsman*.

Edwin Morgan

### The Loch Ness Monster's Song

Sssnnnwhuffffll?
Hnwhuffl hhnnwfl hnfl hfl?
Gdroblboblhobngbl gbl gl gggg glbgl.
Drublhaflablhaflubhafgabhaflhafl fl fl —
gm grawwwww grf grawf awfgm graw gm.
Hovoplodok-doplodovok-plovodokot-doplodokosh?
Splgraw fok fok splgrafhatchgabrlgabrl fok splfok!
Zgra kra gka fok!
Grof grawff gahf?
Gombl mbl bl —
blm plm,
blm plm,
blm, plm,
blp.

Another of Morgan's poems provided an echo of Gysin's permutated poetry technique. But this time the accent in which the poem was delivered was Scottish rather than American, and the theme was musician John Cage's definition of poetry:

'I have nothing to say and I am saying it and that is poetry.'

As Morgan explained: 'This poem, called *Opening the Cage*, might be said to have a musical analogy since it is a set of variations on an initial statement, combining the words to make fourteen other statements that comment upon it.'

Morgan's programme also included an expletive-undeleted poem in which the word 'bloody' occurred continually in a 'tight, bristling' structure of words suggestive of a bees' nest. 'That the bees are Scotch bees,' explained Morgan, 'is indicated by the word "byke" for nest and "bizzing" for buzzing.'

### Bees' Nest

busybykeobloodybizzinbees
bloodybusybykeobizzinbees
bizzinbloodybykeobusybees
busybloodybykeobizzinbees
bloodybykeobusybizzinbees
bizzinbykeobloodybusybees
busybykeobizzinbloodybees
bloodybykeobizzinbusybees
bizzinbusybykeobloodybees
busybizzinbykeobloodybees
bloodybizzinbykeobusybees
bizzinbusybloodybykeobees

If John Cage had nothing to say, programme producer/writer Philip Oxman not only had much to say but also said it in a particularly powerful poetical and dramatic way.

'One of the most way-out and daring things we have ever done' was the way in which Martin Esslin, then Head of Drama, Radio and himself no stranger to experimental radio, described *The Origins of Capital and the Descent of Power*, written by Philip Oxman and made at the Workshop in 1974. It was a programme deeply meshed in symbolism and radiophonic sound, which Oxman himself explained as 'a supposition in dramatic form that the child's quest for origins is addressed not to facts but to myth'.

The script that the Workshop received was like no other they had ever seen. It was typed on graph paper, with accompanying slides. Each actor's voice and sound was meticulously plotted on the grid to enable split-second timing.

Radio 3 Stereo Workshop broadcast *The Origins of Capital and the Descent of Power* in its series of contemporary plays chosen to illustrate new concepts in playwriting. It was certainly a different sort of challenge for Workshop composer Malcolm Clarke who achieved what critic Peter Vansittart later described as 'Voices and sounds that loomed, struck, tottered out of darkness. . . . One was less in a precise story than in a circle of images in words and electronic sound, very deliberately plotted, the relationship between sound and space designed to be as informative as the explicit dialogue'.

Says Malcolm Clarke: Philip Oxman described his play as 'A Circus Piece for Two Sound Sources', and it was an experiment in creating an intricate structure of poetic imagery in words and sounds, rather than telling a dramatic story in the conventional way.

```
(50")                                                                                    oxman
                                    *                                       *
                                                                GIDEON:

                                                                thing I could perform for an enlight-
                                                                ened audience in the public interest
                                                                maybe.

MUSIC OUT                           MUSIC OUT                    MUSIC OUT

WHITE NOISE OUT                     WHITENOISE OUT               WHITE NOISE OUT

EMPTY SOUND                         EMPTY SOUND                  EMPTY SOUND

SCATTERED EXPLOSIVE DAPPLED FIRING ACROSS AUDITIVE HORIZON OF ANIMAL VOICES, BUTCHERY, UNDERGOING TRACKS

MUSIC BEHIND SLOWLY UP              MUSIC BEHIND SLOWLY UP       MUSIC BEHIND SLOWLY UP

TRACKS - - - - - - - - - - - - - - - - - - - - - - - - - - - - - - - - - - - - - - - - - - - (O O

SCATTERED PERCUSSION ACROSS AND UNDER - - - - - - - - - - - - - - - - - - - - - - - - - - - -

unstuck and lost across the auditive landscape and indepth of it):   LAFFY (moving R to C then getting

                                                                "Guff," I said, Neb.
                        I said: Get 'em.
              Get em butt up.
Head-buck butt em gut dead.
                                                                                            Grud!
                            Grud!
                                                            Grud!    Neb.
        My mum's my blood.
Why don't she clean it up?
                                                            By the pure clean  white crime's
                                                            dream sweet birth
                            Why don't she sweep the spit up?
Up Mug!                                                                                      Up Neb!
                Up yours!  Up hers!
                                                     Up and up.
        Love, Laffy.

SILENCE                             SILENCE                     SILENCE
    *3*                                                                                       124"
```

I spent a whole weekend at Oxman's house in the country discussing the piece before we started work on it at Maida Vale. He had conceived it in very precise stereo terms on huge sheets of graph paper, probably 2 feet by 3 feet in size. These were later reduced to more practical proportions. But each of the one inch squares represented a minute in time, with speech and sounds laid out almost like a musical score.

Oxman's story was of a circus family, so poor that they have to butcher the animals that the customers come to see: the sawdust ring is also the sawdust killing floor. The recordings of butchery that were needed for the programme were actually done at the

A small sample of Philip Oxman script for *The Origins of Capital and the Descent of Power*

village butcher's shop near Philip Oxman's home. It was an old-fashioned shop with a slaughter-house round the back. I couldn't bring myself to get involved with that, but I did admire Oxman's style of doing things. He lived near an American Air Force base, and being an American himself rang them up a day or two before he was to record at the butcher's shop and asked them if they would mind not flying loud or low on the recording day. 'Sure,' they said, and everything in the sky was quiet while he got his sounds of meat-saws cutting bone.

After all this poetic and dramatic experimentation, the Workshop composers found themselves with an invitation and a challenge: not to remain purely as collaborators, but also to be originators of their own programmes.

Appropriately, one of the resulting programmes would prove to rank amongst the most successful radio ventures into sound and poetry: Desmond Briscoe's production *A Wall Walks Slowly* which combined Norman Nicholson's poems with the sound of Cumbria, and captured no less than three major awards.

It was Stephen Hearst, then Controller Radio 3, who first encouraged (in 1973) the radiophonic composers of Maida Vale to undertake the occasional individual contribution – of any kind, providing it worked on air. He thus set in train a series of extremely individual contributions to radio which have so far ranged from radiophonic settings of poems to a rock opera.

Something of the character and personal interests of each composer has shown through in what he or she has chosen to do.

The first programme of all – entitled *The Space Between* – was a radiophonic realisation of the Workshop's capabilities. Each member of the staff was encouraged to contribute: their only brief being to make their piece of a suitable length to fit with the others into an hour-long slot.

The programme could very easily have lasted twice as long! Some contributions were never eventually included. David Cain's *Sir Orpheo* was a case in point: too long for the programme, Cain's medieval legend with music was subsequently broadcast as a programme in its own right.

*The Space Between* was reckoned by David Wade of *The Times* to have been perhaps the most ambitious item of the entire Radio 3 Stereo Week. It contained a mix of words and music from electronic sources inspired by jazz, music from natural sound, and animal noises.

One of Malcolm Clarke's contributions to *The Space Between*, which paid tribute to his love of mechanical instruments, was entitled 'La Grande Pièce de la Foire de la Rue Delaware', probably because the title flowed more mellifluously in French than in English. In any case it was a celebration of the home of the Radiophonic Workshop, and the first of twelve pieces which 'set out to entertain rather than inform, and to give some idea of the range of music produced by the Radiophonic Workshop. Later this piece was recorded on a disc called simply: *The Radiophonic Workshop*, the sleeve of which was very Workshop! A colour picture of the interior of Desmond Briscoe's workshop at home, with a synthesiser amongst a debris of workbench paraphernalia.

That the Workshop should come to be so heavily involved in experimental poetry was logical enough: it was, after all, part of the continuing exploration of sound. Such programmes form an important link between the Workshop's involvement with music on the one hand, and words on the other.

Francis Bacon had, of course, previsioned it all in his *New Atlantis*:
Wee represent and imitate all Articulate Sounds and Letters, and the Voices and Notes of Beasts and Birds. . . . Wee have also diverse Strange and Artificiall Eccho's, Reflecting the Voice many times, and as it were Tossing it: And some that give back the Voice Lowder then it come, some Shriller, and some Deeper; Yea some rendring the Voice, Differing in the Letters or Articulate Sound, from that they receyve. . . .

It was an interesting and rewarding period of experimentation for the Workshop's composers. Many strange requests were met with equally strange sounds. Perhaps mercifully, the Maida Vale unit was never asked to undertake a radiophonic answer to that most challenging of all Zen koans:

'What is the sound of one hand clapping?'

# CHAPTER 10
## *The Coming of the Synthesisers*

'The Radiophonic Workshop –
a source of inspiration and experience'
*Dr Robert Moog*

When the Radiophonic Workshop began, the method of working involved firstly the recording of a sound produced either via a microphone i.e. *concrete* or via an electronic generator i.e. electronic. The sound was then manipulated by altering the speed of the tape, filtering, looping, editing, playing it backwards, adding feedback and a host of other *classical* techniques. It took a long time to make even a simple piece of music. In the 'sixties the perfection of voltage control led to the development of the synthesiser and it became possible to create electronic sounds within one piece of equipment and play them in real time on a conventional keyboard, thus producing the music more quickly.
*Simplified description of the Radiophonic Workshop's basic function and facilities.*

The year of the Radiophonic Workshop's tenth birthday, 1968, was notable in many ways, but the most important event was undoubtedly the coming of the synthesisers.

As far back as 1958, when the Workshop was being set up, Robert Moog (to rhyme with Vogue) had delivered a paper on voltage control to the Audio Engineering Society of America – a paper which is now seen to have been the basis of the synthesiser. The Workshop knew of the developments across the Atlantic but nothing was available in Britain until many years later. The first synthesiser that Brian Hodgson knew about was owned by Mick Jagger of the Rolling Stones. 'Brian Jones rang me one day and wanted to come and visit the Workshop, so I said fine. We had a nice chat and he looked around at our equipment and said that he would arrange for me to see Mick's Moog. But somehow it never happened.'

Even when the first synthesisers became commercially available in Britain, the Workshop composers didn't rush out and buy them because they were accustomed to the classic *musique concrète* techniques of tape manipulation and editing. The synthesisers needed an entirely different

attitude, and Brian and Delia were to discover this the hard way.

*Left:* R. A. Moog's Equipment Catalogue
*Right:* The VCS 3. The first British synthesiser

> One night we were completely stunned. We had been trying for ages to achieve what we wanted by the usual means, and it just wasn't happening, Brian remembers. Suddenly the penny dropped. We had our own recently purchased synthesiser that could do it easily. So since the Workshop didn't have one I would bring it in from home to work each day. This soon became a bit embarrassing for the BBC who very shortly afterwards went out and bought two for the unit.

These small synthesisers were known as the VCS 3, and were made by Electronic Music Studios (London) Ltd. They were developed by Peter Zinovieff and the Workshop started working with them officially in 1968. The VCS 3s speeded up the turnaround time for a composition, and soon became very popular with the Workshop composers.

The simplified description of the Workshop's basic function and facilities continues:

> In the Radiophonic Studio, the composer will perform each strand of the music on a synthesiser, the electrical output of which is directly injected into the mixing desk and routed to a single track of the multitrack machine; the process being repeated until the entire piece has been compiled on the different tracks. The

composer will then mix down the piece adding echo and various sound treatments to give the music a semblance of acoustic and add life and sparkle. This operation is often done using a guide track on the multitrack machine to ensure that music and programme fit exactly thus saving time in dubbing theatres and sypher (*sic*) suites later on.

In 1970, two years after the advent of the VCS 3, Desmond Briscoe travelled to Wisconsin University, USA, to lecture on innovative radio at a workshop sponsored by the Corporation for Public Broadcasting and attended by public radio employees from all over America. He took with him the British synthesiser, the VCS 3, and demonstrated its possibilities as an aid in radio productions. He used it extensively in the three projects he directed: a play by Tom Stoppard called *The Dissolution of Dominic Boot*; an audio ornamentation of a poem; and an abstract 'tape poem' in which members of the workshop were invited to interpret the concept of time in a collage of words and natural sounds which they themselves had collected.

Whilst in America, Desmond Briscoe took the opportunity of visiting Robert Moog in New York State to discuss the latest development in Moog synthesisers. Since technology was on the move, he was shopping for the best he could find to equip the Radiophonic Workshop.

At first it looked as though the Moog would fit the bill, but when he returned to Britain Desmond Briscoe discovered that the EMS people had leapt ahead in the technology race by agreeing to produce a much more complex version of the VCS 3 for an East European radio station. This very large and sophisticated equipment was capable of doing all that the Moog Synthesiser could do – and a bit more. It had the additional merit of being British. It was decided that, with suitable modification, the EMS Synthi 100 would suit the Workshop's needs very well indeed.

The BBC agreed, and after all the developments specified by the Workshop had been carried out, delivery was taken of a vast machine which possessed a memory which stored 256 events, and was then probably the most advanced synthesiser in the world. To prepare for its arrival in Delaware Road, Maida Vale, a studio door was widened in record time, and the EMS Synthi 100 – the size of two double wardrobes – was heaved into the Workshop and re-christened The Delaware.

Subsequently the new toy attracted great attention from within and without the BBC. Radio and television producers came to see it and marvel. There was, however, an initial problem to overcome, as Brian Hodgson explains:

When it first arrived and was installed and we were all pleased as anything and longing to get at it, I said to David Cockerell, who had designed it: 'Well, David, where's the instruction manual?' 'Oh,'

replied David, 'you know, we never thought about that.' So David and I sat there for virtually three days and three nights living on steak sandwiches and coffee, writing out a manual. We made a few mistakes, of course, and it was a bit embarrassing later when the Synthi 100 was marketed with a printed and official instruction book: it had a couple of our errors actually printed in!

The now-defunct Delaware – one of the largest voltage-controlled synthesisers ever built

The Delaware reached the pinnacle of its Workshop career when it appeared on the stage of the Royal Festival Hall with Desmond Briscoe in a concert of radiophonic music and sound before a distinguished audience including the Queen and the Duke of Edinburgh.

For years it enabled composers to realise innumerable pieces for radio and TV which would have been impossible by the old methods.

The Delaware revolutionised the way in which some of the radiophonic composers went about their work, and speeded up the process enormously. As is usual, needs gave rise to developments and the Delaware became more and more versatile. But it could also, especially in the earliest days when there was the most interest, be temperamental. On one occasion, Brian was showing it to a group of important people whom the Workshop was eager to impress. It stuck. 'I tried to be cool about it. I patted it gently and said "There, there", and bent forward to jokingly kiss it better. There was a terrible spark and I

Malcolm Clarke in his
revolutionary period during
1974 with the Delaware.
Malcolm's affinity with the
machine is legendary

shot back very un-cool indeed. Later we discovered that the front panels hadn't been earthed and a build-up of static was causing the jam!'

Sadly, the Delaware is no more, having been superseded by smaller and more efficient units. Bits of it have been incorporated into other equipment around the Workshop, but the most important chunks are stored awaiting engineers Ray White and Ray Riley to redevelop it into a worthy successor. It has been suggested that when this project is completed, the new synthesiser should be called The Phoenix.

The simplified description of the Workshop's basic function and facilities concludes thus:

However, the synthesiser only produced electronic sounds and the use of concrete sources diminished as using them involved all the old time-consuming *classical* techniques. Consequently electronic music began to sound rather boring, even at the Radiophonic Workshop. Fortunately technology has now reached an adjacent point on the spiral of development and the computer promises not only to do for concrete sound what the synthesiser did for electronic sound but also to further improve the control of electronic sources.

The acquisition of the Fairlight Computer Musical Instrument has made a tremendous impact on the work of the department, speeding up conventional techniques and allowing development of new ideas previously out of the question because of the pressures of time. The computer-based digital synthesiser is perhaps the most exciting development in electronic music since the invention of the tape-recorder.

The Fairlight had arrived at Maida Vale in October 1981, followed not so long afterwards by one of the men responsible for its development, Australian Kim Ryrie.

As a kid in Sydney, says Ryrie, I was so influenced by the BBC Radiophonic Workshop and its audio magic, both through listening to the radio and watching *Doctor Who* on television, that I had two big and burning ambitions: the first was that one day I would actually visit the Workshop and meet the people who made all those wonderful sounds. The second was to visit Disneyland.

I started to develop the Fairlight in 1975 with Peter Vogel and Anthony Furse. A lot of the early design concepts were mine. It is probably Page Eight which is the most exciting feature of all, representing as it does a full circle back to the very beginnings of radiophonic experiment: the use of natural sounds.

Page Eight helps a composer to 'sample' a natural sound, record it by microphone, and then perform it on a music keyboard. That sound can then be merged by computer with natural or synthesised sound. It is a sound palette designed for musicians and not computer people. The miracles that the Workshop people used to perform with so much painstaking cutting and splicing in the early days can now be done much more easily and quickly. The effect is that you don't have to synthesise a sound but can use a natural sound and blend it and merge it and musically perform the sound in any number of ways – all synchronised to video or film.

There are now a fair number of Fairlights in London, and the people who own them use them in totally different ways. Pop groups like *The Human League*, musicians and composers like Kate Bush and Peter Gabriel. Several British universities have them. In Europe, Fairlights are owned, amongst others, by Jean Michel Jarre and the German group *Kraftwerk*.

Desmond Briscoe adds: There is no doubt that the new generation of computer synthesisers, like the Fairlight, which can provide the composer with immediate performance and control of natural sound, together with a much more flexible means of generating and handling electronic sound is a very considerable step in freeing the creative imagination from the restraints of the equipment – it is people who make music, not machines.

# CHAPTER 11
# *Ingenious Electrical Entertainment*

'The Radiophonic Workshop – Ah yes, *Doctor Who*'
*HM The Queen*

(Ten minutes later)

'Radiophonic Workshop? Ah yes, *Doctor Who*'
*HRH Prince Philip*

---

**'RADIOPHONIC WORKSHOP IN CONCERT'**
*Ingenious Electric Entertainment\**
by the BBC RADIOPHONIC WORKSHOP
*under the patronage of*
MR. JAMES REDMOND, CEng, FIEE, DIRECTOR OF ENGINEERING BBC

| | |
|---|---|
| **Devised Presented and Produced by**<br>MR. DESMOND BRISCOE<br>A popular programme of ELECTRONIC MUSIC<br>supported by<br>THE ELECTRIC INCANDESCENT LAMP<br>THE ELECTRIC CINEMATOGRAPH PROJECTOR<br>THE ELECTRIC MAGIC LANTERN<br>THE MAGNETIC TAPE REPRODUCER<br>**and introducing**<br>THE ELECTRIC VOLTAGE CONTROLLED SYNTHESIZER<br>*The programme will conclude with a piece*<br>*especially composed for the occasion*<br>**'IEE 100'**<br>by MISS DELIA DERBYSHIRE | **The Performance**<br>**under the direction of**<br>MR. BRIAN HODGSON<br>**ably assisted by**<br>MR. MALCOLM CLARKE<br>MR. RICHARD YEOMAN-CLARK<br>MR. PADDY KINGSLAND<br>MR. DICK MILLS<br>MR. JOHN DIXON<br>**in co-operation with**<br>STAFF OF THE ROYAL FESTIVAL HALL<br>AND MANY BBC COLLEAGUES<br>*\*ENTERTAINMENT—a performance which delights* |

*Concerts will be held at 9 pm and also at 10.45 pm*

---

In January, 1971, something obviously important was in the air. Desmond Briscoe had a call from the Director of Engineering, BBC, asking when it would be convenient for him to pay a visit to Maida Vale for a discussion.

By early February, the Workshop staff knew what it was all about. Whereas the Institute of Electrical Engineers always held an annual 'Conversazione' at the Royal Festival Hall, this year was special for two reasons: it was the IEE's centenary, and the Director of Engineering, as a member of the organising committee, had promised that the BBC would put on something quite different from other years; a special entertainment.

'If I can do it *my* way, and can have full support from the BBC lighting and film departments then I'd be only too happy to oblige,' was Desmond Briscoe's reply to the call. Whilst various committees sat and pondered, he scribbled over the front of his minutes for a meeting held in mid-February, the dictionary definition of Entertainment: 'A performance which delights.'

Before such a performance could be conceived in detail, there were 'various and conflicting briefs' that had to be reconciled. A nine-point memo from Desmond Briscoe detailed such necessities as having to appeal to an audience that did not necessarily have 'a thirst for avant-garde music'. The Workshop's contribution would need to be 'visually entertaining and not just a lecture/demonstration', and the concert should 'show something of the nature of the techniques of Electronic music', should not be more than 45 minutes long and is 'to be performed twice between 8.30 p.m. and 11.00 p.m. with at least $\frac{3}{4}$ hour break for a change of audience and the re-setting of equipment'.

Finally it said that 'the calibre of the audience is such that while there is a natural interest in music, electronics and the arts, the social nature of the event and the presence of the ladies, requires that the programme is non-technical, entertaining, aesthetically pleasing and as visually interesting as possible'.

Bearing all this in mind, Desmond Briscoe set out for an Easter weekend trip up-river from his home near Windsor. Mooring his boat by Mapledurham House, he completed the script on Easter Sunday.

The Queen at the Radiophonic Workshop stand at the Royal Festival Hall on 19 May 1971

By 3 May the final arrangements had been agreed, and on Wednesday 19 May 1971 the Radiophonic Workshop was 'In Concert' at the Royal Festival Hall in a spectacular show that included lasers, an appearance on stage of the Delaware Synthesiser, and a powerful PA system that threatened the very fabric of the hall when Delia Derbyshire's specially composed 'IEE 100' included a radiophonic impression of a several times larger than life moon-rocket blast-off! In the galleries, the royal party toured an exhibition which included a Radiophonic Workshop display, with Dick Mills on hand to explain its mysteries.

In between performances Desmond Briscoe was introduced to Her Majesty The Queen, the Duke of Edinburgh and Lord Mountbatten. After assuring Her Majesty that the clouds of coloured smoke hanging over the stage were quite harmless his conversation with the Queen went on for some minutes.

It was a memorable occasion and something of a thrill not only to occupy the Number One Dressing Room at the Royal Festival Hall but also to meet and talk with the royal party, says Desmond Briscoe. But when I arrived at the artist's car park earlier that day I never thought I'd get in. In spite of previous arrangements the car park attendant wouldn't allow me parking space. I finally insisted that if he didn't then it was *his* responsibility if the one solo performer of the evening wasn't there to run the show!

However, the car was parked, the show was rehearsed and at the appointed time the audience arrived. The vast platform of the Royal Festival Hall was occupied by only one large, dimly lit, electronic music synthesiser and six very small synthesisers sitting quietly on a row of chairs; the house lights dimmed and the overture began. An overture accompanied either by film for those parts which originated from television or giant oscilloscope traces in beautiful colours for those items which originated in radio. As the last notes of the overture died away, the small synthesisers blinked into life and performed 'Happy Birthday to You', and the recorded voice of Brian Hodgson filled the Festival Hall with the words, 'Your Majesty, Your Royal Highness, My Lords, Ladies and Gentlemen – Mr Desmond Briscoe.'

Desmond Briscoe who in the darkness had taken his place behind the large Delaware Synthesiser now materialised into the follow spot (an arrangement which he and the operator had come to in rehearsal. Previous attempts to pick him up on a completely black stage had resembled the comic convulsions which occurred in a Christmas pantomime when the 'dame' tried to steal the limelight).

The platform, with all the magnificent woodwork hidden by black drapes was decorated with panels of shiny aluminium, for in order to present the Radiophonic Workshop in Concert, a battery of lighting effects had been supplied by the television service. There was sound operated disco lighting for the 'pop' numbers and a pair of lasers which danced on the large white central screen. Each item of music was accompanied by film or appropriate visual display, whilst simultaneously a series of colour slides illustrated, almost subliminally, the spoken word.

As the applause quietened Desmond Briscoe looked towards the Royal Box:

Good Evening. It is a great honour for the Radiophonic Workshop to be able to salute the IEE on the occasion of its hundredth birthday, for without electrical engineers, there could be no electronic music and without BBC Engineers, no Radiophonic Workshop.

It was our thirteenth birthday last month – on the 1 April! Our overture consisted of familiar pieces for radio and television – maybe you were surprised that some of these were electronic music – but of course you all knew the signature tune for *Doctor Who* – although I doubt if you had ever really heard it before – for most television sets have loudspeakers that are circular and about three inches across, or if you are lucky a little larger and elliptical in shape, and then they are probably looking to the side. In fact, as somebody once said to me, the trouble is with many older television sets, they have loudspeakers looking to the side and those that don't have the screen pointing to the side!

You may have also noticed a familiar rhythm just before the *Chronicle* titles – that rhythm was made for the television service, for use in those days when a clock used to go round in deathly, or was it blessed, silence between the programmes – it became so popular with viewers that it was kept, and only used for breakdowns! It also attracted the attention of some music publishers who asked the BBC if Mr George Martin of EMI could make a Parlophone record out of it – the BBC thought quickly, and a year later said 'yes', and assigned the copyright – that was quite a precedent – the record was called 'Timebeat', a catchy rhythmical piece.

Electronic music is not always like that – one of our first experiments was a 'radiophonic poem' – when we first changed and manipulated sound, and 'tape' meant that for the first time sound became a malleable object, the results were strange and weird, so it is not surprising that this piece was called *Private Dreams and Public Nightmares*.

We also found that the control which magnetic recording tape gave us over sound, meant that we could be amusing as well as frightening, for comedy is a matter of timing and contrast and with sound on tape one can accentuate these parameters. When the Radiophonic Workshop opened, *The Goons* were still going strong, and after long and involved telephone conversations with Mr Spike Milligan, I was determined that we shouldn't just become a goon-show sound-shop – but we did make one sound which has become a Radiophonic classic – 'Major Bloodnok's Stomach'.

The long, loud and very recognisable belch was obviously not electronic and neither is the next piece, but it is music. An excerpt from the score for a television film collaboration with our old friend Ron Grainer who, of course, wrote the *Doctor Who* signature tune, which *is* entirely electronic. This film score is a combination of radiophonic sound and instrumental music – the sound providing the rhythm for the music and also, by manipulation, all the sound effects, for the film *Giants of Steam* – made in the early 1960s, a nostalgic farewell to steam railways.

Also on the subject of transport, music for a television programme on 'do-it-yourself' car maintenance – for this we decided to use the old music hall song 'Get out and Get Under', which seemed singularly appropriate. It was agreed that we should realise it in our terms, but the producer found he had a problem – as you know, the BBC doesn't intentionally advertise, but you can't do a programme on car maintenance without using a real motorcar. It was then agreed with the Society of Motor Manufacturers that a BMC car should be used – but then I think the BBC were worried that BMC would think that the BBC thought that BMC cars sounded like our rather comical 'Family Car'.

So that programme didn't use it! – but it has been used on a number of other occasions. Could the tune be played on a motor horn? Or even on a lot of different motor horns? Or perhaps by recording one real motor horn and playing the tape at different speeds? Not satisfactorily, because when you record a real sound, you also record extraneous sound as well and when you re-pitch the sound to get different notes, other things, like bird song or traffic hum make themselves evident, so in fact we 'synthesised' the sound of a motor horn. Real sounds can, however, be recorded and played at different speeds to produce a tune, but the result is often comic, if not ludicrous, as in our 'Christmas Commercial', 'O Come all ye Faithful', played on a cash register.

The bell played the tune whilst the drawer noise provided the accompaniment. However, if you take a truly pleasant sound and the one I have in mind is that which is produced by hitting the neck of an empty wine bottle with the palm of the hand when you get a very small sound, 'bloop'. If we tune this, by changing tape

The original cash register

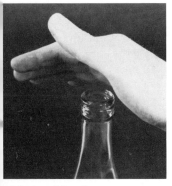

Making a 'bloop'

speed, over say three chromatic octaves, you have a whole orchestra of bloops from great big fat long 'bloooomps' to little thin high 'bleeps'. The tune can now be written to synchronise with the graphic design of the title film for a consumer research programme *Choice*. A complete piece made from one Sauterne bottle in B flat! It is unusual to find a natural sound source that is actually on a note; we have in one of our studios a fire extinguisher marked approximately G sharp; I don't know if it has yet featured in a composition! It is also relevant that *Choice* was made from a Sauterne bottle, for when you strike the neck, you are exciting a resonant cavity – if it were a Beaujolais bottle then, of course, the sediment trap would give a different shaped cavity. Differently shaped bottles give different sounds.

Electronic sound, from oscillators, or tone generators, can be shaped and formed to provide a score for the television film *The Bridge*, a film about architecture and the engineer, Ove Arup. The same technique can be used to realise a completely different, abstract, piece, *The Delian Mode*.

Over the years we have done many pieces of work for the local radio stations, and some of these were put, under various new titles, on a long-playing gramophone record called *BBC Radiophonic Music*; tracks from this record are sometimes used for programmes when there isn't time to compose and realise something specially; recently, a young lady from television schools department telephoned, saying she wanted some music to go with a film of the stars in the heavens. I suggested the record, thinking of various possible tracks, including *The Delian Mode*. However, the next day, she telephoned again to say that they had

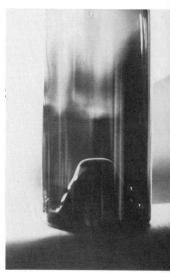

used the track called 'Milky Way'. I thanked her and thought –
now what was that for originality? – ah yes, the East Anglian
programme *Dairy Farming Today*!

Music for BBC Local Radio Station, Radio Leeds, Women's
Programme, also had its title changed and, made from a rhythm of
door knockers accompanying a chorus of door bells, is now known
as 'Door to Door'.

People have always expected the Radiophonic Workshop to be
filled with modern sophisticated equipment, but until quite
recently, special equipment for electronic music just did not exist;
we used as sound sources whatever came to hand; our
harmonium, which we use occasionally as a source of sound, had
engraved in brass on the one pedal the date 1887 and on the other
pedal 'Mouse-Proof Pedals'. Surely we are the only department in
the BBC with mouse-proof pedals. But we are also 'with it' – as
illustrated by our music for the pop programme, *Scene & Heard*.

The voltage controlled synthesiser has its place in pop music
but for this occasion my colleague Miss Delia Derbyshire has
composed a piece *IEE 100* which was realised with the help of BBC
Archive recordings and the EMS Synthi 100 known to us as the
Delaware. The theme is the history of electricity in communications; the musical form and rhythm are based on the
morse for IEE, which is in fact rather dull until you add the full-
stops. You will hear the voices of Mr Gladstone congratulating Mr
Eddison, the opening and closing of BBC Savoy Hill and astronaut
Neil Armstrong stepping on to the moon. Ladies and Gentlemen,
it is my pleasure to conclude our programme with 'IEE 100'.

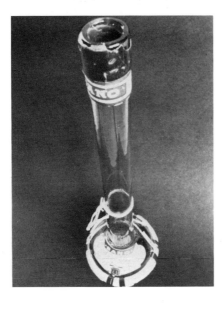

*Far left:* The Sauterne bottle in B
flat, give or take a swallow

*Centre left:* Fire extinguisher in G
sharp

Each bottle makes a different
note

# CHAPTER 11
## *Hitch-hiking on...*

'Nothing, really, is impossible. If the idea is there,
then the rest will follow'
*Desmond Briscoe*

*Doctor Who* just happens to be the longest-running science fiction series
that the Workshop has tackled. There have been a multitude of others
of the same genre, from *Quatermass and the Pit* in the early days through
space-oddities and encounters with Triffids, Kraken, Robots, Elves and
Mutants and also the hairy-footed Hobbits of Middle Earth who,
understandably, love beer and songs.

Elizabeth Parker was involved for two-and-a-half years providing the
radiophonic sound for *Blake's Seven*. The incidental music was composed
by Dudley Simpson, but Elizabeth still found herself fully stretched.

Gareth Thomas (left) as Blake
and Paul Darrow as Avon with
Decimas in *Blake's Seven*

I usually prefer to use basic natural sounds, and mix them and make them work. That's my pet enjoyment. But on *Blake's Seven*, of course, most of the sounds would never be heard in real life. So I concentrated on making my 'spacey' sounds as interesting as I could. Buttons being pushed didn't just go 'Beep'. Explosions didn't go 'Bang'. I could have achieved those sort of sounds through a synthesiser more easily: but what I chose to do was to combine electronic sounds and tape manipulation in order to give them texture.

The texture of a towel is another matter entirely. In only one popular science-fiction series has the hero relied so massively on such an everyday object. It is, according to the author: 'The most useful thing that any interstellar hitch-hiker can carry.' There are no prizes for guessing the name of the series.

A legend in its own time, *The Hitch-Hiker's Guide to the Galaxy* started off modestly enough in 1978 on Radio 4, describing itself as 'perhaps the most remarkable, certainly the most successful book ever to come out of the great publishing corporations of Ursa Minor', and claiming that it had already supplanted the great 'Encyclopaedia Galactica' as the 'standard repository of all knowledge and wisdom' among the more relaxed civilisations on the outer eastern rim of the Galaxy.

Its motto, which was Don't Panic, would be an appropriate one for the Workshop.

*The Hitch-Hiker* was obviously just the thing for the Workshop, and sure enough the programme producer was soon round at Maida Vale shopping for rockets firing, winds howling, earthquakes wiping out prehistoric landscapes complete with animals, volcanoes erupting and giant boulders cracking open and turning into spaceships.

'Yes, sure, that's okay,' replied Paddy Kingsland, 'anything else?' Of course there was something else – quite a lot of something else.

The comedy radio series quickly became a cult television series . . . a popular set of records . . . a play . . . a book . . . and generally a way of life, featuring, amongst other characters, the two-headed Zaphod Beeblebrox, the man once voted 'the worst dressed sentient being in the Universe'.

'Oh yes,' said the producer, 'and we will also need the sound of an office building flying through space in the grip of seven powerful tractor beams, and treatment to make actors' voices sound slimy and robotic.'

Undaunted, Paddy Kingsland took note of what was needed and so began a long-running relationship with Arthur Dent and Ford Prefect and all the other characters of a series that so rapidly became a cult. He even remained cheerful whilst spending hours in the company of Marvin, the manically depressed robot.

*The Hitch-Hiker* possessed a link with *Doctor Who* quite apart from the fact that both series are 'spacey': writer Douglas Adams was also script editor for the good Doctor.

Paddy Kingsland: When *The Hitch-Hiker's Guide to the Galaxy* came along I thought that it was ideal, not only something I could enjoy doing, but something really suited to the Workshop since it needed so many of the things that the department had, and was good at: special equipment, the right atmosphere, people with feeling, flair and time to apply themselves wholeheartedly within the time available.

Mark Wing-Davey as Zaphod Beeblebrox and Sandra Dickinson as Trillion from *The Hitch-Hiker's Guide to the Galaxy*

I had known Simon Brett, the producer, before, and he brought along Douglas Adams, who had written the series. Both of them knew the Workshop and its potential for jiggery-pokery, and thought that *The Hitch-Hiker* was ideal Workshop material, which, of course, it was.

We had to prove ourselves with a pilot programme, which immediately got off the ground. Then I did the sound for the first six programmes, though not the music which was provided from discs. Then there was a Christmas Special, for which I wrote the incidental music as well as the special sounds.

The next set of programmes – five in all, bringing the series to a total of twelve episodes – was broadcast over one week. Since the scripts didn't arrive until the last minute, I found myself working day and night. By the Monday we had only two programmes ready for broadcasting. I actually enjoy working like that, but there's no denying it was a chore. When the scripts demanded robots talking to humans, the treatments needed just the right balance otherwise Ford Prefect would talk like a robot and the robots like people. We put all the voice-lines onto multi-track and had the whole thing to bits more than once in order to get it right.

Despite the problems, *The Hitch-Hiker's Guide to the Galaxy* was great for me in that it had a wide public appeal. Many of the programmes I had previously worked on were marvellous in themselves but limited in their appeal to the public. Like *Doctor Who*, *The Hitch-Hiker* captured the general imagination and became a sort of cult, not only here but also in America, where the series was broadcast later. Again, this was very good for me in that I was invited to visit the USA for a radio convention, Foundation for Radio, on the strength of *The Hitch-Hiker's Guide to the Galaxy*.

The TV version needed an entirely different approach. For instance, when I ended the world on radio, I ended it *my* way. On television I had to match my sounds to various visuals: to the control-room of the Vogon space-ship launching the ultimate destructive weapon, to the different reactions of people on earth as the place blew apart.

Though creating the end of the world was a bit complicated, other effects for *The Hitch-Hiker* were comparatively simple. For instance, we had some limping robots that I achieved rather neatly, I thought, by getting someone to walk around with his foot in a wastepaper basket.

I even got to play a part in the series: as a talking door, saying 'Have a Nice Day'.

The Workshop gained a decided boost in morale in 1976 when BBC Radio set up a committee which surprised everyone by not being yet another talking shop, but a committee empowered to put money on the line if, after discussion, a programme was considered worth making.

It was called the Creative Radio Committee, a title that offended many people, and was therefore toned down to the Feature Workshop Committee. Its philosophy was to make programmes to an open deadline with a built-in 'right to fail'.

The Workshop, thus empowered, set out on two programmes which – far from failing – captured no less than four awards out of a possible 10 from the Society of Authors Awards for Radio in 1977.

Desmond Briscoe was not only delighted that his own programme *A Wall Walks Slowly* and Malcolm Clarke's *August 2026* had done so well, but hoped that the added prestige for the Workshop might create a more sympathetic attitude when he next passed round the begging bowl for funds for more facilities.

In 1977 a small booklet of Norman Nicholson's poems, together with photographs of tapestries made by an old gentleman in the North East of England, was the inspiration for *A Wall Walks Slowly*. The booklet, called *Stitch and Stone*, caught Briscoe's imagination since he had always had a great love of Cumbria and was fascinated by the musicality of the people's speech. He thought: This could be radio – the tapestry could be sound. 'So I went to see Norman Nicholson,' said Desmond Briscoe, 'and he read me some of his poems, and I knew that with his strong themes of weather, walls and sheep, I could present the landscape of Cumbria. The programme's sub-title was in fact "The Sound of Cumbria".'

The resulting programme was made largely without compromise, inch by inch, and when first transmitted it produced an enthusiastic response from the public. At the Society of Authors Awards for Radio in 1977, *The Times* radio critic David Wade reported:

Anyone who heard Desmond Briscoe's *A Wall Walks Slowly* will agree that it was worth a prize: it got one for 'outstanding production or direction'. Maybe it was worth two prizes: it got two – the second being as a 'documentary feature'. Was it worth three prizes? Three is what it took, because the Gold Award for 'the single most outstanding contribution to radio' also went its way.

I have neither the space nor the nerve to catalogue the competition yet again, so must ask you to take my word for it that, considering what there was – anyway in the first two categories – this splendid portrait of Cumbria was in quite a different class from the rest of the opposition. So yes, *A Wall Walks Slowly* was worth three prizes: but in this sweeping triumph you should also read a message not very flattering to the rest of radio as well as a suggestion from the jury that more work of this type and standard badly needs to be produced.

Desmond Briscoe: I was extremely lucky in that one of my contributors to the programme, the Chief Ranger of the Cumbrian National Park – John Wyatt – is a writer himself, a lover of the Lake District and its wildlife. His contribution was not only his own naturally poetic speech on almost any subject, but his ability to take myself and the engineer to the places where we needed to go to record the water, and the wildlife, even the much promised buzzard that never actually appeared.

Back at the workshop I worked on the tapes I had made, extracting the words I wanted and polishing and cutting in order to get the rhythms and shapes and phrases right. Then we divided them into categories – weather, sheep, walls and so on. At that time only were they transcribed to paper – we had done everything from the actual spoken interviews so far, which is not the usual way to work.

It was a slow process. Having built up my speech track and integrated the poetry in the right places, I then had to create the sound picture, using as raw material all the natural sound I had recorded in Cumbria. At this stage I was joined by one of my staff – Peter Howell – who, to put it mildly, is a very sympathetic pair of ears. Also he is a very exacting critic but one of those people who have the ability to understand what I was trying to do. Under Peter's hands it all came to life and everything I wanted to achieve he managed to produce out of the material that was available.

Peter also wrote the music, because there was no indigenous music that I could use; 'John Peel' played on a few accordions was not what I was after.

Val Arnold-Foster wrote in the *Manchester Guardian*:

It was both God's and Man's landscape: brooks and birds, farms and small grey towns, a landscape to be considered in detail. Norman Nicholson is a writer absorbed by depiction, who notices the lichen as he does the high crags. He knows his countryside with an almost obsessive intimacy and describes the dry stone walls of his title not only as a poet, but as a craftsman. He was therefore an excellent choice for this programme, which set out to produce a portrait.

Painting with words is a challenge to producers and writers in the non-visual medium of radio. What is needed is a definite structure of content and form, though sometimes what we get is a confused amalgam of words and music. Here the structure was provided by the verse – each poem dealing with a different aspect of country and small town life – as the programme moved down from the fells to the farmlands, the quarries and the iron ore workings to the seashore. The editing has to be disciplined. The producer, Desmond Briscoe, who also did the interviewing, must have discarded hour on hour of rural material for later programme makers.

*A Wall Walks Slowly* emerged as a beautifully knit piece, using sound effects and some particularly sympathetic music for oboe and cor anglais with discretion. For each poem there was an antiphon of local voices, sometimes reinforcing, sometimes expanding the poet's theme.

Ray Bradbury's chilling story *There Will Come Soft Rains* has had the benefit of the Workshop's special sounds in three separate productions. The first occasion was a production by Nesta Pain in the 1960s with music by Antony Hopkins. Then came a version for schools by Dickon Reed. The third was unusual not only in itself, but also for the fact that the Workshop's *equipment* gained top billing in the programme credits:

*August 2026* by Ray Bradbury, 'There Will Come Soft Rains', adapted for Narrator, Vocoder and Synthesiser by Malcolm Clarke.

The programme broadcast in 1977 was a personal triumph for Malcolm Clarke, who created all the music and all the sound and, as Desmond Briscoe remarked 'practically everything else as well'. It won him the Award for Best Drama Adaptation in the 1977 Society of Authors Radio Awards presentation.

It was the first time that vocoder and synthesiser had been used to such an extent in radio drama. They proved an ideal way to realise Bradbury's story of a single all-electronic robot home, with built-in cook, maid and nanny, which continues its ritual even though the people it used to care for are no more than images baked on the outside wall by a nuclear blast.

Paul Ferris in *The Observer* wrote: 'Beautifully done, with the Radiophonic Workshop at full stretch, illustrating Bradbury's elegant conceits. SF, so difficult to realise on film, is ideal for radio, which characteristically, hardly touches it, preferring famous trials or the lives of the great poisoners.'

An entirely different venture for the Workshop was a radio feature involving a poetic putting-together of words, music and sounds. Desmond Briscoe's *Narrow Boats* was a nostalgic look at the life gone by of people living and working on England's inland waterways. Broadcast in 1977, it had already been available on record for seven years – firstly on the BBC Records label when it was nominated by the *Daily Telegraph* as 'Speech Record of the Year', and then later on the Argo label.

*Narrow Boats* attempted to capture in words, sound and music something of the disappearing world of the 'narrow boat', and of the people whose lives were entirely bound to the boats and canals on which they worked and travelled. Desmond Briscoe, himself a keen explorer of the inland waterways of Britain, arrived with his tape-recorder in the nick of time to preserve the voices and stories of boatmen, lock-keepers, lengthmen, toll-keepers and others. Many of the people he interviewed had died before the programme was broadcast. The music was not – for a change – produced electronically, but sung and played by David Blagrove, a schoolteacher whose life-long obsession with the canals and the people of 'the cut' had led him to write many songs about the narrow boat people.

These songs, together with the recordings that Desmond Briscoe had captured up and down the waterway network of the British Isles, were subtly merged with BBC Archive material using the full resources of the Radiophonic Workshop. The resulting poetical blend of natural sound and the speech of ordinary people, together with the folk-type songs, was something that had not been heard on radio since Charles Parker made his famous Radio Ballads.

Desmond Briscoe traces his influences in making the programme to the time that he was on a BBC Staff Training Course where he first heard the work of Denis Mitchell.

Ted Livesey opened my ears to the contents of the BBC Archives and I used to listen to the fascinating things I found there and be completely entranced – but for the terribly pompous BBC interviewers who, every time they spoke, killed the whole thing dead.

Denis Mitchell, who was a radio features producer in Manchester, long since moved into the wider world of television, was for me the first BBC person to take his tape-recorder out into the streets and get real people saying things which he would then use. Later, Charles Parker abstracted by tape editing an essential and poetic authenticity from actuality interviews. I first travelled on a canal in the early 'fifties and during the middle 'sixties I realised that there was a world full of exciting sounds which just didn't occur elsewhere – the extraordinary syncopated rhythms of two-stroke diesel engines, the noises made by sluices, and all the other wide range of watery sounds.

The programme actually arose out of a need by BBC Records for a follow-up disc to a record they had made of railway sounds. Narrow Boats neatly fitted this requirement.

The making of Narrow Boats is an example of the subtleties of programme making at the Radiophonic Workshop. It doesn't sound as if it was made at the Workshop, people have said, forgetting that the unit's output of background manipulation of sound to achieve subtle effects is as great as its 'spacey' and nightmare creations.

Desmond Briscoe: It was made at the Workshop because there are very talented people there and many facilities for changing acoustics on words, cutting tape in order to shape it and alter it and make rhythms fit the songs. Once sound is on tape it is malleable: that fact was the *raison d'être* for the Workshop in the first place, and we are experts in doing all sorts of things with tape.

So when, for instance, we go under a canal bridge in *Narrow Boats*, or go through a tunnel, we don't have to say it, we just change the acoustic. Again, most of the songs were recorded in a canal village in the Midlands in a cottage where there was certainly no diesel engine, and I needed one in the background. Even if there had been an engine there it would not have matched the rhythms. But in the Workshop, all of these things can be manipulated and treated.

*     *     *

Music in the act of making . . . the aural stimulation of the imagination . . . when does sound become music? . . . why aren't words enough? Over the years, the Radiophonic Workshop has tackled many aspects of musicology.

*Glyndebourne – an Opera in Preparation*, was devised and produced in 1976 by Peter Howell, who had himself worked at the Opera House in Sussex for four years at the beginning of his career, mostly as an assistant stage manager working with sound.

His programme, realised at the Workshop, was an impression of life in and around Glyndebourne, and was drawn from the voices and sounds recorded during the preparation for the 1976 production of *The Marriage of Figaro*, exploring the techniques and artistic skills involved in presenting an opera to the public.

*From Hand to Mouth*, written and presented by Philip Oxman in 1978, used myth, music and the physiology of hearing to make 'an exploration of desire and its instruments in the working life of humankind'.

With an illustrated introduction by A. L. Lloyd, the programme was realised at the Workshop by Philip Oxman, Malcolm Clarke and Bill Aitken and produced by Desmond Briscoe in 1978. The hypothesis that this programme was based on was that 'All animals always hear. To hear is the fundamental involuntary activity that initiates experience of the outside world. But hearing is not listening. Only when the flow of hearing is interrupted by attention does listening occur. There must be *desire*' (Philip Oxman).

*Don't Move the Paper Any More* was described in *The Times* as 'Radio Triumphant'. An hour-long feature written by Philip Oxman and produced at the Workshop in 1981 by Piers Plowright and Malcolm Clarke, it was about a French-Israeli ethno-musicologist, Simha Arom, attempting to understand and transcribe the weird music of central African tribesmen.

To a background of throbbing drums and the vocal counterpoint of pygmies, Arom shuffled his sheets of music paper back and forth in an attempt to work out how the separate musical lines related to one another. 'Don't move the paper any more' was the cry. So Arom didn't, and discovered that the time had come to abandon the abstraction of theory, and just play.

Anne Karpf wrote: 'The programme escaped the predictable sandwich – speech, music, speech – which often turns features into lectures. Instead, the music whispered to you softly from some inner chamber in your ear, and then crept out to displace the central position of the words. Sounds dripped into the programme, and were truly mixed.'

It was a programme not only about music, but – as *The Times* commented: 'A journey deep into one man's musical ethos, with marvellously coloured pictures and unnervingly strange sounds at every bend of the road.'

Also in 1981 a musical programme of an entirely different kind was *It Was In Tune When I Bought It*, which featured Peter Townshend, of the Who, and Hank Marvin, of The Shadows, in what the *Radio Times* called 'a beguiling and contrasted reminiscence of their experience with the guitar'.

'Give any kid a chord book and a guitar, and he'll play. That's one of the great things about it. It liberates music,' said Pete Townshend. During the programme he confessed that since he doesn't have a natural ability for solos and 'got frustrated because I couldn't play the way I wanted to', he went in for visual impact to 'get the attention I wanted'.

Hank Marvin's approach was more dulcet, though he still craved a visual image. Twenty years or more ago he bought an American Sunburst Stratocaster – a flamingo-pink instrument that impressed the fans: 'When I flashed it around the clubs in London,' says Hank, 'people would just ogle it with their tongues hanging out.'

The programme was made by Paddy Kingsland, himself a guitarist, together with Harry Parker. The two composers constructed out of the two separate conversations with Townshend and Marvin an hour of recollection, illustration and cross-reference which (said the *Daily Telegraph*) 'was not only a delight to hear but lit up, too, twenty-five years of social, musical and broadcasting history'.

In 1979, a musical called *Rockoco* was a unique programme for the Workshop. Though the department had been involved across a wide range of different programmes, from concrete poetry to full orchestral works, it had never before tackled a major pop/rock musical. The programme came about after Managing Director Radio, Aubrey Singer, had asked for 'blockbuster' ideas.

Paddy Kingsland, who had been experimenting with Geoff Shankley on a rock musical, promptly sent off tapes of the songs and an outline of the story.

Other BBC management heard the tapes and liked them and finally the programme was accepted. Paddy immediately contracted arranger Anthony Bowles, who had worked on *Jesus Christ – Superstar* and *Evita*, and an impressive cast of singers – many of them from West End musicals. *Rockoco* was a full-scale musical production. Says Paddy: 'I enjoyed the experience – but perhaps on reflection it didn't really come off. It gained a big "E" for Effort, but if I were to do it again, then I would have to work up a stronger story line.'

It was a great achievement on Paddy's part, comments Desmond Briscoe, not the least part of which was persuading Radio to pay for it. It must have been one of the most expensive things of its kind that the BBC has ever done. Certainly it was the first time that we used our 16-track machine which in fact arrived just in time to be temporarily installed in Studio 6, Maida Vale, for the recording of the orchestral and vocal tracks. Then the whole thing was brought to Paddy's studio in order to put the programme together.

A surreal world where characters are larger than life – the world of *Rockoco*

*Concerto for Orchestra*, written and produced by Desmond Briscoe, was 'an impressionistic view of the BBC Symphony Orchestra drawn from its members past and present'.

When Controller Radio 3, Stephen Hearst, wanted a major music feature about the orchestra from the inside, Desmond Briscoe decided to use the Bartók Concerto for Orchestra as a 'vehicle' – because of the way it is orchestrated – and to interview some twenty members of the orchestra on their life and work, the pattern of the questioning being derived from the moods of the five movements of the work.

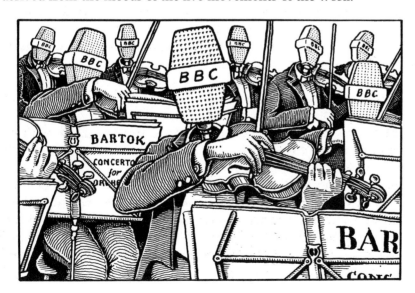

The views of BBC Symphony players interwoven with Bartók's music in *Concerto for Orchestra*

'Their words were intercut and fitted to the tempo, rhythm, mood and phrasing of the music, which had been recorded with binaural pairs of microphones over each section of the orchestra in order that when any one member was speaking, the listener was hearing the orchestra from that point of view. It was a little like trying to make an opera when someone else had written the music and a whole group of people were contributing the words.'

When I discussed with the members of the orchestra the best way of getting a really excellent performance of the work in a studio situation (rather than a concert hall), it was unanimously agreed that Pierre Boulez should be the conductor. Knowing of his interest in sound, I approached him – and indeed he did come over to conduct a most exhilarating performance which we recorded from the Symphony Orchestra studio up to the 16-track recording machine in the Radiophonic Workshop's Studio E.

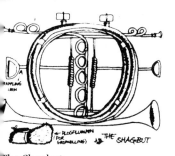

The Shagbut

Broadcast in 1980 *Concerto for Orchestra* was specially recorded so that the listener could hear the orchestral passages 'from the front' and also have an impression of the subtle differences in the sound normally heard by each musician. Each surrounded by his own individual environment of sound, the musicians, as they played, voiced their thoughts on the life of a symphony player and on the music as they hear it.

'Whilst there were purists who complained, feeling strongly that "words" should not be put over such music,' says Desmond Briscoe, 'the resulting programme was greatly appreciated by members of the music profession and, indeed, members of the orchestra thought that it should be compulsory listening for all non-orchestral musicians.'

The Minikin

Back in 1968 the Workshop welcomed three instruments which had never quite made the grade. They were featured in a Radio 3 programme by Michael Mason entitled *The Shagbut, the Minikin, and the Flemish Clacket* . . . for such were their names.

Francis Bacon, who had written in 1624 of 'Diverse Instruments of Musick likewise to you unknowne', would have despaired.

The Shagbut was described in the programme as 'a two-man trombone, formed mainly of boiled leather and twenty-five feet of tubing. Neither aesthetically pleasing, nor practical'.

The Minikin was referred to as 'a sort of arthritic virginal, with its mechanism taking exactly a minute from keyboard to string, mainly because the instrument was six yards long'. There was, quite naturally, a time lapse before the Minikin could give forth its rather plingy sound – and it filled this with a 'ratchety-gratchety' coughing and spluttering.

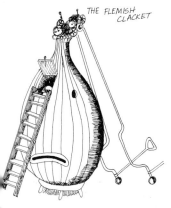

The Flemish Clacket

The bass line was provided by the Flemish Clacket – a lute of the larger sort. Apparently it was some fifty feet in height! Since it didn't possess a fingerboard, it was played from the inside, with the tuner outside.

The final performance of the concert proved a little too much for the players. The Minikin duly went 'ratchet-gratchet-ratchet' for exactly sixty seconds before becoming 'little and plingy' . . . the Flemish Clacket boomed on with the Shagbut until the musicians and the piece they were playing just collapsed in a heap.

Could this, listeners wondered, be a musical spoof?

Indeed it was, realised at the Workshop by programme producer Michael Mason with the help of composer David Cain, a firm fan of *most* medieval instruments other than the Shagbut, Minikin and Flemish Clacket.

*    *    *

The Radiophonic Workshop came of age on 1 April 1979, the event being marked by five radio and television programmes, a mention in Hansard (Philip Whitehead, MP for Derby North: 'In which the hon. Member for Aldershot and myself . . . are locked in an awful radiophonic workshop in the sky. . . .'), a large party at the Langham Gallery, features on radio stations throughout the country, appearances on *Nationwide* and *Pebble Mill* and in the major television documentary *The New Sound of Music*, a BBC LP *Radiophonic Workshop* and a poem by composer Carey Blyton.

**Sound Also the Wee Houses** *by Carey Blyton*
Toil, toil, toil and trouble,
Sound of cauldron, sound of bubble;
Sound of Doctor Who in space,
Rescuing the human race;
Sound of viscera in revolt –
Done with just 1 millivolt!
Sound of fishes in the sea –
Off the shelf, no extra fee!
Sound of toilets flushing madly,
Sound of beetle weeping sadly;
Sound of Maida Vale Canteen
(*Ghastly* things behind the scene);
Sound of phagocytes at large,
Ploughing through some ancient marg;
Sound of Desmond going bonkers
As he trips on several conkers
Used upon a cornflake packet
To produce a fearful racket;
Sound of Dick Mills hard at work
As he makes sounds for some burk
Who's hoping *all* he'll much surprise
(And carry off the Italia prize);

Sound of Paddy, John and Peter
Doing strange things with a tweeter –
Sound of Brian, Liz and Roger
Making 'horrors' for *The Lodger*;

What would we do without their noises?
IT'S WORK FOR *MEN*, AND NOT FOR BOISES!

HAPPY 21ST BIRTHDAY TO THE RADIOPHONIC
WORKSHOP!

When Desmond Briscoe took the idea of a radio feature which looked at the work of the department, and also the nature of the aural stimulation of the imagination, to Stephen Hearst, Controller Radio 3, the reply was: 'Yes, but surely there are two programmes here?' Ultimately, indeed, there were two programmes. *We Have Also Soundhouses . . .*, subtitled 'The Craft and Art of the Radiophonic Workshop', surveyed the department's origins and development, and contained excerpts from many of the pieces referred to in this book, from *Private Dreams and Public Nightmares* to *The Greenwich Chorus*. The contributors' credit list was a distinguished roll-call of radio and television producers, writers and critics; plus radiophonic composers, past and present, talking about their work.

Devised by Desmond Briscoe, and compiled and introduced by Michael Smee, the programme was produced by David Rayvern Allen. The same team also wrote and introduced the second birthday programme, *Sound In Mind*, which was an investigation of the aural stimulation of the imagination, produced by Desmond Briscoe.

The BBC Radiophonic Workshop celebrates its 21st birthday with a survey of its origins and development: *We Have Also Sound-houses . . .*

The programme started by asking four questions:
How does sound act on the brain?
When does sound become music?
Why aren't words enough?
How dependent on association is evocation?
With the help of creative broadcasters, critics, radiophonic composers and a man blind from birth, the programme then attempted to answer them.

These people were interviewed by writer Michael Smee for both programmes and some of them expressed themselves as follows:

*Michael Bakewell*
*Producer, Radio & TV*
Once we realised what could be done with sound, all its other uses immediately occurred to us. Desmond Briscoe also had very considerable musical abilities which gave us a headlong start because the more we began to tinker with sound, the more we realised that some kind of musical knowledge was going to be essential.

Other people came in . . . Daphne Oram had a particularly sharp musical sense and I think that most of the other people who were recruited after them were recruited as much for their dramatic abilities as their music.

*Donald McWhinnie*
*Producer, Radio & TV*
When you are producing a radio programme you use all the ingredients economically, with discretion, and every sound has a purpose. . . .

*Raymond Raikes*
*Producer, Radio Drama (retired)*
In radio, which is purely non-visual, radiophonics are enormously powerful; the fact that they are very nightmarish and out of this world can be of enormous value, but they are completely lacking in soul and passion and the things that really go to make drama.

*David Lyttle*
*Senior Producer, Schools Radio (retired)*
Schools are some of the best customers of the Radiophonic Workshop because we are working for an audience of children, and radiophonic sound in so many ways lends itself to the work we do, not only in terms of surrealist sound effects, but in music as well. Not just signature tunes but whole suites of music find their way into the programmes and every new schools producer is given an introduction to the uses of the Workshop as early as possible.

*Philip Saville*
*Producer/Director, Television*
When I go into the Radiophonic Workshop I feel that I'm in *real* territory . . . as opposed to the so-called real territories in life which I feel are unreal. In the so-called real world there are omissions and restrictions and rigidities, when you go to the Radiophonic Workshop they start with the purpose of making something unreal, and therefore it can only grow more real. I think that you can paint in sound. I have used the Workshop quite extensively in terms of misplaced sanity.

I heard a programme the other day, *A Wall Walks Slowly*, which was written and directed in such a way that it made an incredible quilt that was of reality but deeply poetical, though not in a pretentious way at all. Just the poetry of life, really, it reminded me tremendously of being alive.

*Frederick Bradnum*
*Writer and Producer*
One of the snares about radiophonic work is that it automatically fits into dream elements; it automatically fits into that area of unconsciousness, of things that one is either dreaming about, day-dreaming or properly dreaming, or in that in-between state.

*André Molyneaux*
*Television Producer/Director*
The great joy of the Radiophonic Workshop is that you do exactly the same as you do with any composer: you look at the film together and you tell him where you would like the music, and he makes suggestions.

I only ask for something. I cannot overestimate what they do. I think that their composition is wonderful . . . that combination of composer, musician and engineer seems to me to be an amazing skill.

Schools Television has used them a great deal, partly because of the flexibility, partly because they will do things quickly and sometimes because, if you are doing something on money or coins, you have only to mention that to them and they will immediately think of using coins themselves in the music.

*Molly Cox*
*Television Director*
Years ago, when I did radio sound effects, I can remember Lance Sieveking asking me to give him a 'blue' sound to be in a creepy play. We didn't have the technical ability to make a blue sound then – now the Workshop would ask: 'What colour blue?'

*David Wade*
*Writer and Critic*
I remember putting in a script of my own, 'At this point there is a cosmic scream'. And, well, we got a cosmic scream. The sound is creating something that is not actually describable in words, and that's the point of it. If it could be described in words, why use the sound?

*Vera Gray*
*Producer, Schools Radio*
Whenever I wanted the idea of strange fantastic shapes, or strange movements as of a giant's seven league strides in his seven league boots, I found that whereas before I had been using musical instruments to create everything, the radiophonic sound could create something which was even more fascinating.

*Molly Cox*
One of the virtues of radiophonic music is that it isn't corny, that is to say that unlike film music . . . or the mood music library which gets a lot of uses . . . it is always spanking new. Even sounds that have never existed before. They are manufacturing something absolutely fresh so that it may have references back to real noises (just as an abstract painting has references back to painting with figures in) but is a completely new sound, there's nothing boring about it.

*          *          *

Another programme which had an instant appeal was 'an evocation of Orkney, drawn from the poems of George Mackay Brown, the sound of Orkney, and the thoughts of the Orcadian people'.

*The Poet in His Place* was broadcast in 1981 to mark the poet's sixtieth birthday. Afterwards George Mackay Brown wrote to Desmond Briscoe, who wrote and produced the programme: 'I withdrew from the birthday party last night and retired to the kitchen to hear in (almost) privacy, our programme. I am deeply moved, and grateful, that you should have chosen to broadcast that marvellous mosaic on my birthday.'

George Mackay Brown, a poet who has never travelled as far south as England, was chosen by Briscoe as the basis for a radio programme because he felt there was so much in his work that could be linked with the people of the surrounding community. Also, Briscoe believes that the more isolated communities, such as Cumbria or Orkney, still retain a natural eloquence which is not easily found in what he describes as 'the debased language of the 1980s'.

With the help of Radio Orkney's far-from-soundproof studio, and in the teeth of the ever-blowing Orcadian winds, Briscoe brought back a total of over twenty hours of interviews, weather noises, and Orcadian sounds. 'Quite often we would be recording in Radio Orkney when the local hotel closed – noisily. We were certainly well entertained by the local people with their home-brewed ale, and though I was not privileged to actually attend a wedding in Orkney, I did manage to record the entire repertoire of six excellent local fiddle players and sufficient background party noises to create the sound of such an occasion.'

He recorded the sounds of the weather, sea, birds and the voice of the poet reading his poems. The Orcadians talked about their environment in the poetry of everyday speech – 'on a good summer's day, you can see the edge of the world' – grouping them round themes like drinking, fishing and music.

Back at the Radiophonic Workshop he blended these field recordings in a carefully constructed mosaic where each voice had its own position in the stereo picture, with single sentences abstracted from different speakers in a context 'where even the platitudes sound meaningful'.

The programme was popular with listeners and with the critics. Anne Karpf remarked in *The Listener* that 'Briscoe is in love with sound. . . . He has inherited the mantle of the late Charles Parker, and has polished up a style which demands obsessive perfectionism, and produces little works of art'.

David Wade in *The Times* looked back over the year of broadcasting and singled out *The Poet in His Place*. 'It is only in such rare programmes that the art of fine documentary feature-making on Radio 3 was kept alive'.

A programme which no radio listener has yet heard was made in 1980.

It was called *The Snail is Jammed Again*, and was a send-up of the type of avant-garde radio programme that features a string quartet, solemn poet and lady soprano. The programme was also supposedly made at an inopportune time: when the Americans were apparently invading Britain and getting ever closer to the BBC Studios at Maida Vale.

*The Snail is Jammed Again* was produced by Desmond Briscoe, who says: It had an interesting score and was beautifully performed, but it was only mildly funny – and no one has so far plucked up sufficient courage to suggest that it should be broadcast. It certainly was a most interesting – if exhausting – exercise, since we did all the studio work in one very long day, and mixed it down later. Those of us here in the Workshop who were involved will never forget the bizarre scenes of getting our lady soprano to sing down a piece of plastic drainpipe, while we worried about how to obtain the right snail-like quality for her voice!

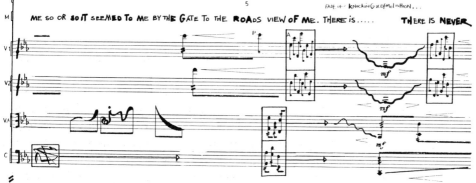

*Left and above: The Snail is
Jammed Again*

Perhaps it will make a 1 April broadcast on the Workshop's
birthday some year, but it might be best to consider it as an
example of the experimenter's 'right to fail'.

The ability to create a snail-like noise is not among the qualifications
required from a Radiophonic Workshop composer, and neither is a
knowledge of brain surgery. Both, presumably, come under the blanket
heading 'the ability to interpret programme requirements when the
subjects are outside the composer's own previous experience'.

Certainly Peter Howell never thought when he first joined the
Workshop team that he would enrich his own knowledge of medical
science. Yet in the course of his work, Peter experienced an intensive
year-and-a-bit with Jonathan Miller's *The Body in Question* during
which he says he almost *became* the body in question.

Following this, he found himself coping with seven films exploring
the human brain, its biological make-up and all the areas of its activity,
for *The Human Brain* on BBC 2.

Like Paddy Kingsland before him, Peter combined orchestral
instruments with electronics to realise the music he wanted. Thus, in
Peter's radiophonic terms: The human brain means viola and
synthesisers.

Whilst Peter Howell was working on *The Body in Question*, another Workshop composer, Richard Yeoman-Clark, was weaving together the sounds of the human body itself into a programme called *A Symphony of the Body*.

The music for *The Body in Question* blocked the BBC switchboard for two days with callers asking where they could buy the record, while *The Symphony of the Body* stopped composer Antony Hopkins when he was driving in his car. 'I found it so spell-binding that I was compelled to sit in my car on a very cold night for at least twenty minutes listening to a programme that I could simply not switch off.'

Meanwhile – for such is the lot of the Radiophonic Workshop – the unit continued its past/present relationship: on the one hand continuing to produce the dinosaur noises requested of it over the years, and on the other to look forward to the future with Brian Hodgson assisting Jonathan Harvey in his realisation of the *Seven* (an important radio version of *Seven Against Thebes*), and two programmes which may be major radio events of 1983: Peter Howell's radiophonic treatment of Dante in his own *Inferno Revisited*, and Desmond Briscoe's programme about the poet Charles Causley in his Cornish town of Launceston: *By St Thomas's Water* – a portrait drawn from the poems of Charles Causley and the thoughts of some thirty of his friends and acquaintances, including academics, schoolteachers, sailors, journalists, radio producers, a retired farmer, a retired traffic warden, a vet and a poet. Their words are woven into a setting which illuminates both the man and his poetry.

*       *       *

Finally, a question: What do the following literary works have in common?
*Hamlet, Alice in Wonderland, The Day of the Triffids, The Cherry Orchard, Macbeth*
According to the Radiophonic Workshop staff they were all definitely written with the Workshop in mind. No doubt about it!

Certainly they are ideal for radiophonic treatment and certainly they have cropped up again and again over the years in versions for radio or television. No one would be at all surprised if next week's requests included yet another for the unit to weave its radiophonic magic on the play that superstitious actors refuse even to name, calling it instead 'the Scottish play'.

If *Macbeth* should turn up again, then composer Roger Limb would prefer someone else to tackle it. His version proved only *too* successful, and remains an example of the remarkable power of radiophonic evocation and atmosphere.

Tradition has it that Shakespeare knew what he was writing about when he gave the witches their lines, and that his spells really did work.

Therefore, the canny actor always leaves a bit out, just to be on the safe side. When Roger Limb tackled the witches scene, he gave it the full radiophonic works: voice treatments, supernatural jangles, in short, all the weird and wonderful effects that the Workshop does so well.

So well, in fact, that he couldn't bear to hear it again.

'When the producer came to hear the tape,' says Roger, 'I gave it to him and switched on the machine:

"Would you mind playing this while I go and have a coffee," I asked him. "It's nine minutes long and it frightens me to death."

When I came back ten minutes later the producer was waiting there, very pleased – but very very pale!'

# Appendix 1

**Workshop Creative Staff**

Over the past 25 years many people have learned from and contributed artistically to the Radiophonic Workshop; amongst those who have served three months or more are the following:

| | *Joined in the year* | | *Joined in the year* |
|---|---|---|---|
| Daphne Oram | 1958 | Sue Cassini | 1974 |
| Desmond Briscoe | 1958 | John Taylor | 1975 |
| Jimmy Burnett | 1958 | Trina Hughes | 1975 |
| Dick Mills | 1958 | Roger Fenby | 1976 |
| Dennis Morgan | 1959 | Alistair Wilson | 1976 |
| Phil Young | 1959 | Val Doulton | 1977 |
| Geoffrey Smith | 1959 | Bill Aitken | 1977 |
| John Harrison | 1960 | Elizabeth Parker | 1978 |
| Maddalena Fagandini | 1960 | Chris Lewis | 1977 |
| Geoff Leonard | 1960 | Jeremy Birchall | 1977 |
| Norman Bain | 1960 | John Downer | 1977 |
| Charles Clark-Maxwell | 1961 | Harry Parker | 1978 |
| Jenyth Worsley | 1961 | Richard Atkinson | 1978 |
| Delia Derbyshire | 1962 | Colin Beaumont | 1980 |
| Brian Hodgson | 1962 | David Hitchinson | 1980 |
| John Baker | 1963 | Clare Elstow | 1980 |
| Margaret Etall | 1963 | Helen Halliday | 1980 |
| Anthony Askew | 1964 | Amanda Alexander | 1980 |
| Keith Salmon | 1965 | Isobel Sargent | 1980 |
| Janet Gibson | 1965 | Graham Puddifoot | 1981 |
| Bridget Marrow | 1965 | Gill Pell-Hiley | 1981 |
| Roger Charlton | 1966 | Mark Farrar | 1981 |
| Clive Webster | 1966 | Stuart Robinson | 1981 |
| David Cain | 1967 | Jonathan Gibbs | 1981 |
| Malcolm Clarke | 1969 | Mike Shilling | 1981 |
| Paddy Kingsland | 1970 | Diana Howell | 1981 |
| Richard Yeoman-Clark | 1970 | Bob Coles | 1982 |
| Norman McLeod | 1971 | Sue Thomas | 1982 |
| Lloyd Silverthorn | 1971 | James Birtwistle | 1982 |
| Roger Limb | 1972 | Alison Taylor | 1982 |
| Glynis Jones | 1972 | Anna Antoskiewicz | 1982 |
| Pete Dixon | 1972 | Simon Clifford | 1982 |
| Peter Howell | 1974 | John Walley | 1982 |

# *Appendix 2*

**Workshop Equipment 1982**

*Studio A*

| | |
|---|---|
| Synthesisers | PPG Wave 2-2 |
| | Roland 100M |
| Treatment Equipment | EMS Vocoder |
| | Audio Design Recording Compex Limiter F760-RS |
| | Roland CSQ 100 Sequencer |
| Mixing Desk | Soundcraft Series 800. 26 into 8 |
| Submixer | Roland SMX 880 Line Mixer |
| Multitrack Tape-Recorder | Soundcraft SCM 8 track |
| $\frac{1}{4}$" Tape-Recorders | 2 Studer A80 RC. Stereo |
| | 1 Revox A700. Stereo |
| Noise Reduction | BEL BC3 |
| Speakers | BBC LS 5/8 |
| Echo | Great British Spring |

*Studio B*

| | |
|---|---|
| Synthesisers | Yamaha CS80 |
| | ARP Oddessey |
| Treatment Equipment | Deltalab DL4 Digital Delay Line |
| | Eventide 910 Harmoniser |
| | Audio Design Recording Limiter Compressor F760XRS |
| | Roland SPH 323 Phase Shifter |
| | Roland SEQ 315 Graphic Equaliser |
| | Roland SBF 325 Stereo Flanger |
| Mixing Desk | Soundcraft 1624. 24 into 16 |
| Submixer | Roland SMX 880 Line Mixer |
| Multitrack Tape-Recorder | 1 Studer A80 16 track |
| $\frac{1}{4}$" Tape Recorders | 2 Studer A80 RC. Stereo |
| | 1 Revox A700. Stereo |
| Noise Reduction | BEL BC3 |
| Speakers | BBC LS 5/8 |
| Echo | EMT Stereo Plate |

*Studio C*

| | |
|---|---|
| Synthesisers | Prophet Five |
| | Casiotone 201 |
| | Yamaha SY2 |
| | Yamaha C15 |
| Treatment Equipment | Roland SEQ 315 Graphic Equaliser |
| | Roland SPH 323 Phase Shifter |
| | Roland SDD 320 Dimension D. Spreader |
| | MXR Pitch Transposer |
| Mixing Desk | Soundcraft Series II. 16 into 8 |
| Multitrack Tape Recorder | Studer A80 8 track |
| ¼″ Tape Recorders | 2 Studer A80 RC. Stereo |
| | 1 Revox A700. Stereo |
| Noise Reduction | BEL BC3 |
| Speakers | BBC LS 5/8 |
| Echo | Roland 301 Chorus Echo |
| | EMT 262 Gold Foil Plate |

*Studio D*

| | |
|---|---|
| Synthesisers | Roland 100M |
| | Wasp Deluxe |
| Treatment Equipment | Albis ⅓ Octave Filter |
| | Deltalab DL4 Digital Delay Line |
| | Roland SP 355 Pitch to Voltage Synthesiser |
| | Roland SBF 325 Stereo Flanger |
| Mixing Desk | Soundcraft 1624. 24 into 16 |
| Submixer | Roland SMX 880 Line Mixer |
| Multitrack Tape Recorder | Studer A80 8 track |
| ¼″ Tape Recorders | 1 Studer B62. Stereo |
| | 1 Studer B62. Twintrack |
| | 1 Revox A700. Stereo |
| Speakers | BBC LS 5/8 |
| Echo | AKG BX20 |
| | Great British Spring |
| | Roland RV 800 Spring |

*Studio E*

| | |
|---|---|
| Synthesisers | Oberheim OBX 8 |
| | Yamaha SY2 |
| | ARP Oddessey |
| Treatment Equipment | Eventide 949 Harmoniser |
| | Countryman Phaser |
| | Korg Rhythm 55 |

| Mixing Desk | NEVE 8066. 20 into 16 |
|---|---|
| Multitrack Tape Recorder | Studer A80 16 track |
| ¼″ Tape Recorders | 2 Studer A80 RC. Stereo |
| | 1 Revox A700. Stereo |
| Noise Reduction | BEL BC3 |
| Speakers | BBC LS 5/8 |
| Echo | EMT Stereo Plate |
| | Local Echo Room |

*Studio F*
1 16mm 6 Plate Steenbeck Viewing Console
1 16mm Sonder Libra MO3. Magnetic Track Recorder
1 Studer A80 RC Twintrack Tape Recorder
1 Roger Sharland Multi Duty Counter Timer

*Studio G*
1 16mm 4 Plate Steenbeck Viewing Console
1 Acmade Picture Synchroniser

*Studio H*

| Synthesisers | Roland Jupiter 4 |
|---|---|
| | Yamaha CS 40 M |
| | Roland 100M |
| Treatment Equipment | Roland SVC 350 Vocoder |
| | Roland PH380 Stereo Phaser |
| | Roland CR78 Compurhythm |
| Mixing Desk | Soundcraft Series II. 16 into 8 |
| Submixer | Roland SMX 80 Line Mixer |
| Multitrack Tape Recorder | Soundcraft SCM 8 track |
| ¼″ Tape Recorders | 1 Studer B62. Twintrack |
| | 1 Studer B62. Stereo |
| | 1 Revox A700 |
| Speakers | BBC LS 5/8 |
| Echo | Great British Spring |

In addition to VHS video viewing machines in each studio there is a Fairlight Computer Music instrument, a set of Custombuilt Wavemaker Oscillator, Filter and Envelope shaping modules with digital polyphonic keyboard and control voltage recorder and two Radiophonic Workshop Time Code Reader Memory Units. These items are booked and moved from studio to studio as necessary.

# *Appendix 3*

## WORKSHOP RECORDS

DR WHO ...........................................................................RES L 11
FOURTH DIMENSION............................................RED 93 S
MOONBASE 3.............................................................RES L 13
DIAL M FOR MURDER..............................................RES L 20
THE RADIOPHONIC WORKSHOP .....................REC 196 Stereo
BBC RADIOPHONIC MUSIC...................................REC 25M
OUT OF THIS WORLD ..............................................REC 225 Stereo
MUSIC FROM 'THE CHANGES'...............................RESL 33
THE EARLY MUSIC CONSORT OF LONDON........REC 91 Stereo
    (David Cain: The Hobbit, The Jew of Malta,
              Much Ado About Nothing and Hajji Baba.)
THROUGH A GLASS DARKLY ................................REC 307
THE ASTRONAUTS and MAGENTA COURT ........RESL 53
    (from 'Through A Glass Darkly')
SOUND EFFECTS No. 19 'DOCTOR WHO'..............REC 316
RADIOPHONIC WORKSHOP 21 ............................REC 354
DR WHO SIG. (NEW ARRANGEMENT) ...............RESL 80
DR WHO The Music......................................................REH 462
SOUND HOUSE..............................................................REC 467

# Index

## Acknowledgements

STEVE BENBOW/NETWORK pages 8, 15, 46 bottom right, 50 both pictures, 72, 75, 92, 96, 99, 100, 105; BRIAN BERESFORD/TUSHITA STUDIOS page 115; MALCOLM CLARKE pages 16 both pictures, 78 bottom, 128 right, 137 both pictures, 138 all pictures, 139 both pictures; BOB COBBING page 116; DICK MILLS page 46 top, 51; MARK GUDGEON page 79 top; INSTITUTION OF ELECTRICAL ENGINEERS page 134; E. MORGAN page 122; RADIO TIMES pages 150 top, drawings by Will Hill, bottom Ellis Nadler, 153 Will Hill; CHRIS WARE for BBC pages 26, 40, 44, 46 bottom left, 58 both pictures, 65, 67, 73, 111. Drawing by PAUL JOHNSON, pages 158–159; Drawings by MICHAEL MASON page 151; Graph with permission from PHILIP OXMAN, page 124; JENYTH WORSLEY page 29 top; NORMAN BAIN page 77. The remaining photographs are BBC copyright.

'The Loch Ness Monster's Song' and 'Bees' Nest' with permission from EDWIN MORGAN and CARCANET PRESS. 'I am that I am' with permission from BRION GYSIN and JOHN CALDER (Publishers) Ltd. A.R.T.H.U.R. with permission from LAURENCE LERNER and THE HARVESTER PRESS LTD; 'Relativity' with permission from LILY GREENHAM; page 38, letter to *The Listener* quoted with permission from SPIKE MILLIGAN; *Sound also the Wee Houses* by Carey Blyton, page 152.